Don't Take No For An Answer

Don't Take No For An Answer

The 2011 referendum and the future of electoral reform

Lewis Baston and Ken Ritchie

Biteback Publishing

First published in Great Britain in 2011 by
Biteback Publishing Ltd
Westminster Tower
3 Albert Embankment
London
SE1 7SP

ISBN 978-1-84954-207-4

10 9 8 7 6 5 4 3 2 1

A CIP catalogue record for this book is available from the British Library.

Printed and bound in Great Britain by
CPI Group (UK) Ltd, Croydon, CR0 4YY

Contents

Acknowledgements   vi

Introduction   ix

1. The Long Road to Electoral Reform   1
2. The Referendum Campaign   21
3. The Dimensions of a Disaster   44
4. Why AV was Always Going to   58
     Lose the Referendum
5. Why Yes Lost Quite So Badly   75
6. 'Once in a Generation'?   101
7. The Art of the Possible   111
8. A Winnable Reform   131
9. The Next Steps   156

Conclusions   176

Appendix   181

Acknowledgements

Eric Heffer's memoirs were entitled *Never a Yes Man* – many colleagues thought the publishers had accidentally omitted the subtitle *Always a Grumpy Old Sod*. I was a Yes man, at the end of the Alternative Vote (AV) referendum campaign, but I was a grumpy old sod as well. I was unenthusiastic about the choice of AV or FPTP, depressed by the banality and stupidity of the referendum campaign and very uncertain as to whether AV was in the long run interests of my position on electoral systems (pro PR) or my party preference (Labour). These perspectives inform the contents of this book, although I hope that people coming from other perspectives (Yes and No on AV, Lib Dem, Conservative and other parties, and supporters of FPTP and AV) can find things with which to agree or engage in constructively.

In writing about the referendum, anyone must be grateful for several rapidly produced insider accounts. The key text was produced by Andy May, but other fascinating contributions have been produced by James Graham, Jessica Asato, Cory Hazlehurst and John Strafford from the Yes side, and Tim Montgomerie and Dan Hodges from the No side. Peter Kellner of YouGov has helped in providing and analysing polling data. Thanks also to various people (Yes, No and neutral) who read and commented on the text anonymously, and to my colleagues and friends at Democratic Audit for their forbearance about this outside interest.

Iain Dale, of Biteback, demonstrated yet again why he is the most innovative publisher in politics (and probably in general) by taking on this book at very short notice and doing the seemingly impossible. I am very grateful to him and his team for what they have accomplished. Hollie Teague deserves a particular mention for coping with my sometimes recherché use of metaphor.

The production of this book has been supported by Aharon Nathan. The contents of the book, though, reflect my own views rather than his, and he has never asked for more than a fair hearing for his own preferred electoral system ('Total Representation' – TR). His main interest in supporting me has been to ensure that the lessons of the referendum are learned and that thinking begins about how to change our electoral system, an idealistic and unselfish aim I share.

It was one of my tasks when I worked for the Electoral Reform Society to consider what I politely called 'variant electoral systems' submitted by members of the public to the ERS. Most of these were ingenious but unworkable in practical terms, and a few of them were entertainingly eccentric or belonged inside 'green ink' territory. I developed a natural resistance to people who had bright ideas about new voting systems, and it took some charm and persistence for Aharon to get through this barrier. But his TR system is simple, intuitive and different enough from AV to get around some of the problems which derailed that electoral system in the referendum. It deserves consideration as a reform option that would be a feasible step forward for the UK electoral system.

Another huge debt is to Ken Ritchie, Chief Executive of the ERS during my time there as a member of staff. Ken's service to the cause of electoral reform has been enormous, and he remains a passionate and thoroughgoing advocate of reform, democracy and human rights. Ken, unlike me, was an active supporter of a Yes vote in the referendum and worked selflessly for that cause. He has helped massively with the writing of this book, drafting several sections and offering constructive comments throughout the process. He deserves credit as co-author. I should also note that Ken has at several stages urged me to be more generous-spirited about the Liberal Democrats, and about our former colleagues in the Yes campaign; if this book has the occasional hint for the Yes campaign of 'good cop bad cop', Ken is the good cop. I hope the result combines justice and mercy in appropriate measures.

This book is dedicated to my wise mentor and kind friend, Sir David Butler. Anyone who writes about British elections owes David a huge debt.

Lewis Baston (principal author)
August 2011

Introduction

Nothing can disguise the fact that the May 2011 referendum was an appalling defeat for electoral reform. The campaign for the Alternative Vote (AV) was not just beaten, but absolutely trounced. Only a few months before the referendum the Yes campaign was enjoying a small lead in the opinion polls, but by the time it came to polling day more than two-thirds of voters (67.9 per cent) threw out the proposal for change, and in only ten of the 440 counting areas did the Yes side win.

This book tells the story of that referendum. It is not, however, simply an historical account of what happened – it is also an attempt to understand how a campaign that had so much enthusiasm and goodwill on its side slumped so disastrously when it came to the final weeks before polling day.

We as electoral reformers were, like many others, bitterly disappointed by the outcome, but we see defeat not just as an unfortunate accident or a consequence of the stupidity of the electorate but as the result of the way the campaign was planned and fought. Our analysis might not make comfortable reading for those who led it and we take no satisfaction in criticising their decisions and actions. They were for the most part good, well-intentioned people – many of them friends and former colleagues – but we owe to them, and the thousands of people around the country who campaigned for change, our explanation of why things went so badly wrong and the chance to change the voting system was lost.

Some have maintained that we are unlikely to get another opportunity to reform the electoral system for a generation. We do not take such a gloomy view, but for us the greater danger is that should another opportunity arise we will again blow it. We therefore need to understand why we lost, what we did that should have been done differently, and what we need to do the next time. The work that went into the Yes campaign will not have been entirely in vain if we are able to learn from it and ensure that we are better prepared to fight the next referendum, whenever it might be.

This book is therefore not just about the past but about the future. What can we do to create the circumstances in which electoral reform will return to the political agenda? How can we engineer a referendum, or indeed another route to reform, that is winnable? How then should we run the campaign to achieve the outcome we want?

These are difficult times for electoral reformers. Many are not just disappointed but demoralised and despondent. Some point with anger at the dishonesty and disingenuousness of the No campaign. That is understandable, but the cause of electoral reform demands that we make an honest assessment of what went wrong and recommit ourselves to the work that lies ahead.

AV was never a system that was on its own going to transform politics in the way that a more proportional system, which most reformers wanted, would have done, but it was a system that would at least have ameliorated some of the worst features of FPTP. AV might have been, in Nick Clegg's infamous words, 'a miserable little compromise' but reformers had some justification in claiming it to be a small step in the right direction.

The referendum on AV was a dismal failure, but that does not mean we should now just sit back and accept FPTP as an inevitable part of our electoral arrangements. FPTP remains a quite dysfunctional system – an affront to our democracy. We cannot simply regard it as an accepted feature of our elections that cannot be changed: those who have campaigned, in many cases over many years and even decades, for something better must now take stock of the new situation and plan where we go from here. This book is about how we can do that. We offer no easy answers and no instant solutions, but history reminds us that the demand for electoral reform has been around for 150 years and has survived many setbacks, and it tells us that nothing is impossible.

Chapter 1

The Long Road to Electoral Reform

The referendum of May 2011 was an historic event. It was only the second national referendum in the history of the United Kingdom. It was the culmination of many decades of campaigning and research by supporters of electoral reform – a chance at last for the people to make a choice about the electoral system. And it was a shattering defeat for electoral reform.

Despite the disaster, it is not the end. The cause has travelled a long road which has had more than its share of twists and turns. There is still some chance of seeing the replacement to the House of Lords elected by a system that represents the diversity of views and choices among the electorate. The concept of electoral reform for the House of Commons will be back before very long, even if the 2011 referendum has closed off many choices. If the reform case is made in better circumstances, with a more robust option on the table than AV proved to be in 2011, and a more competent campaign, it can still win. The struggle goes on, but in order to win in future the electoral reform movement has to face up to and absorb the lessons of what happened in 2010–11 and not seek false comfort.

The Origins of Electoral Reform
The idea of improving democracy by changing the electoral system has been around in British politics since at least the 1860s. Thomas Hare wrote then about the iniquities of an

electoral system that produced so many safe seats, prevented the best candidates from winning and distorted the popular will. He could not then have foreseen that a century and a half later we would still be facing the same problems. And when John Stuart Mill championed Hare's idea for a better voting system, which later developed into the Single Transferable Vote (STV), he would not have known just how long reform would take in coming. However, reflecting on just how long the demand for a fairer voting system has been around, and on how the movement for reform has survived despite so many setbacks, should help us put the disappointment of the referendum result into some perspective. History tells us that a defeat is not the end of the story.

Things of course have changed since the time of Hare and Mill. The Reform Acts of the nineteenth century expanded the franchise and the campaign for women's suffrage eventually triumphed. Even the voting system has undergone changes: the multi-member constituencies, some of which survived to 1950, and the 'university seats' being elected by STV, have disappeared, and between 1867 and 1885 some seats were elected by the 'limited vote' system which offered minority parties a better chance of gaining representation. In the 1920s the Northern Ireland Parliament and local authorities were elected using STV, but the system was abolished to cement the unionist ascendancy in place – STV did not return to the province until the 1970s. Serious change in Great Britain did not arrive, however, until the Labour government of 1997 which gave us proportional systems for devolved levels of government and a limited form of preference voting for mayors. However, that is jumping ahead in our story.

In the early years of the twentieth century, the newly

formed Labour Party could clearly see the need for electoral reform. Keir Hardie, the father of the Labour Party, and other founding members knew that social justice and democratic fairness must go hand in hand, and in 1913 their Independent Labour Party voted almost unanimously for proportional representation. But it was not just the ILP that wanted a change in the voting system: in 1911 the TUC voted for electoral reform and in 1912 the Scottish TUC resolved that:

> no scheme of Electoral Reform could be considered that does not include Proportional Representation.

Perhaps it was democratic idealism and perhaps it was a realisation that only through a fairer voting system could they expand working people's representation in Parliament. Then, as now, it is when principle and self-interest coincide that we are most likely to see progress.

As Labour gained in strength, however, its commitment to electoral reform began to wane, but not before the Alternative Vote (AV) entered the field as a new competitor. Parliament debated it in 1918 and, with Labour support, the Commons passed it. The Lords, however, wanted to go all the way to STV, which is the proportional version of AV, and so nothing changed. The debate continued through the 1920s until in 1931, under a Labour government, the Commons again voted for AV but on that occasion the government fell before it could be enacted. In a mirror image of this process, the Liberal Party's interest in electoral reform increased as it sank from being one of the major parties of state into minority status.

The Wilderness Years 1931–83
After the election of 1931, electoral reform was off the

agenda for more than forty years. FPTP, according to the classic academic 'law' of Maurice Duverger, promotes two-party politics and that is what we got. The Liberals were reduced to a fringe party and until 1970 the Conservatives and Labour together won around 90 per cent of the votes: not until 1997 did their combined share of seats drop below 90 per cent. Even in 1951 when Labour had its highest ever share of the votes – 48.8 per cent to the Conservatives' 48.0 per cent – but lost the election there was no serious challenge to the voting system.

The Heath government was willing to introduce STV as part of the political process in the troubled province of Northern Ireland, but despite lip service to unionism most politicians saw the place as essentially foreign. Though constitutional fixes were considered necessary they were not seen as having any relevance to institutions on the other side of the Irish Sea.

However, the turbulent politics of the 1970s did put electoral reform on the agenda again. The two-party duopoly of votes collapsed abruptly in the February 1974 election, with the Liberals surging to 19.3 per cent of the vote but winning a ludicrously unfair fourteen seats in the Commons. The Conservative and Labour votes both slumped to 37–38 per cent; the Conservatives polled slightly more votes but the result was a hung parliament with Labour just ahead on seats. It was the first hung parliament since 1929–31.

There was a brief period in which the outgoing Prime Minister Edward Heath and Liberal leader Jeremy Thorpe discussed possible electoral reform, but it proved impossible to do a deal. Part of the reason was that Heath's best offer – a Speaker's Conference – was not enough for the Liberals.

But the election result was such that neither a combination of the Conservatives and Liberals, nor a Labour–Liberal tie-up, had a majority in Parliament.

After a few months of minority government, Labour squeaked to victory in the second 1974 election with a majority of three – 50.2 per cent of the seats – but still did not climb above 40 per cent of the vote. The Conservative outcry that followed the February election led to the creation of Conservative Action for Electoral Reform (CAER), with many prominent Conservatives such as Robert Carr, Douglas Hurd and Chris Patten as members. Alas, however, Tory indignation was short-lived and CAER soon shrank to the handful of members it has today. The Liberals were also unsuccessful in persuading parliament to adopt PR for the new European Parliament elections.

The electoral upheavals of 1974, the rise of the Liberals and the nationalists in Scotland and Wales, and the detachment of Northern Ireland from the electoral politics of Britain were not an aberration but a lasting change. Even in 1979 the reversion to two-party politics was superficial, with the Liberals maintaining a higher vote than in any 1931–74 election despite the adverse circumstances, and the combined two-party share being just over 80 per cent rather than the habitual 85–95 per cent of other post-war elections.

Labour's Awakening 1983–96

The 1983 general election provided another major shock to the system. Labour, in disarray and having suffered defections to the new SDP, had its lowest share of the vote since 1918 – only 27.6 per cent. The Liberal–SDP Alliance was narrowly behind on 25.4 per cent, but FPTP nevertheless gave Labour 209 seats and only twenty-three to the Alliance, surely one of the worst distortions that FPTP has ever produced. The result might have given Labour a good reason for wanting to retain FPTP, but it had more problems ahead.

In the 1987 election Labour, with a new dynamic leader in Neil Kinnock, barely passed 30 per cent of the vote and questions were being asked over whether Labour could ever win again. Fear of perpetual opposition provided Labour's small band of electoral reformers with an opportunity to begin the debate in the party. LCER, the Labour Campaign for Electoral Reform, started to grow, with a powerful champion in Robin Cook.[1]

By 1990 Labour had set up a commission to examine the case for a change in the voting system. The Plant Commission, under the chair of Professor (now Lord) Raymond Plant, however, had a hard job. Its members, leading party and trade union figures, were split on the issue. Neil Kinnock became gradually more sympathetic to reform, but could not square the internal politics of the party in time for a coherent position to emerge in time for the 1992 election. While the party tried to convey open-mindedness, it seemed to many electors to be more like muddle, and the Conservative counter-attack in the last week of the election featured attacks on electoral reform.

When the Plant Commission eventually reported after the 1992 election, it rejected proportional representation but, by a small majority, recommended a change to what they termed the Supplementary Vote (SV), the system now used for mayoral elections. Although the system was already in use for presidential elections in Sri Lanka (and has a familial relationship with the French presidential electoral

---

1 See Martin Linton and Mary Georghiou (Southcott), *Labour's Road to Electoral Reform* (LCER, 1993).

system), the then Labour MP Dale Campbell-Savours was credited for devising this compromise. By this time John Smith – perhaps not an ideological electoral reformer but certainly a sincere democrat and critic of the current arrangement – had taken over as Labour leader and he committed the party to a referendum on the voting system.

Towards the referendum 1996–2008

The process that led to the AV referendum began in earnest in 1996. Although Labour was riding high in the opinion polls, with the Conservatives still suffering from the disastrous events of Black Wednesday (16 September 1992 when the pound had to be withdrawn from the European Exchange Rate Mechanism), Labour was taking no chances. A deal was struck with the Liberal Democrats through the Cook–Maclennan talks whereby in exchange for Liberal Democrat support in the event of a hung parliament, Labour would promise a referendum on a new voting system drawn up by an independent commission. There was a broad agreement on constitutional reform such as devolution and human rights between the two parties.

When the election came the following year, Labour won a landslide victory, even if only on 43 per cent of the votes. To its credit, it set about a programme of constitutional change the likes of which had never been seen before. Within months of taking office it had legislated for the referendums which would lead to the Scottish Parliament and Welsh Assembly, with the London and Northern Ireland Assemblies to follow – all elected by proportional systems. It also introduced a proportional system for electing MEPs, and the Supplementary Vote for electing mayors.

The big change that Labour had offered was, however,

the chance to reform the voting system for the Commons. By the end of 1997 a commission had been formed with Lord (Roy) Jenkins as chair. Its remit was:

› to consider and recommend any appropriate system or combination of systems in recommending an alternative to the present system for parliamentary elections to be put before the people in the government's referendum;
› to observe the requirement for broad proportionality, the need for stable government, an extension of voter choice and the maintenance of a link between MPs and geographical constituencies.

Electoral reformers could hardly have asked for more – and this from Labour, a party that had shown no enthusiasm for electoral reform since the days of Keir Hardie. A referendum on real change seemed to be just around the corner, and the reform community immediately got to work planning the campaign they assumed they would soon be fighting. The Make Votes Count (MVC) coalition was formed with generous support from the Rowntree Reform Trust, bringing together the key campaign organisations – the Electoral Reform Society (ERS), Charter88, the Fawcett Society, and the New Politics Network – and a cross-party group of leading politicians, including Charles Kennedy, Bob MacLennan and Chris Rennard for the Liberal Democrats and Stephen Twigg and Martin Linton for Labour. It was later to be chaired by David (now Lord) Lipsey of Labour who had been a member of the Jenkins Commission.

The following year the Commission completed its work, recommending a newly devised system, the Alternative Vote Plus, or AV+. It entailed the election of 80–85 per cent of

MPs in single-member constituencies using AV, but with the remainder of MPs elected in wider areas to compensate for the disproportionality which AV could produce. These 'additional' members were to be elected by giving electors a second 'party' vote using a semi-open-list system (in which voters could opt simply for a party list or for a particular candidate on a list).

Although AV+ was welcomed by the great majority of reformers, there was some disappointment that the commission had not gone for STV, which seemed the obvious way towards a broadly proportional system, gave voters more choice and involved geographical constituencies. Moreover, AV+, with its mix of preference voting (i.e. the ranking of candidates in the AV contests) and semi-open list system, appeared worryingly complicated, and to implement it without increasing the number of MPs would require substantial redrawing of constituency boundaries. Nevertheless, it was recognised that AV+ was on the agenda and that it represented the best chance of ditching FPTP. Even when the ERS, which was committed to STV by its then constitution, conducted a ballot of its members, 88 per cent called on the Society to campaign for AV+, although it proved a divisive issue.

However, by the time of Labour's autumn 1998 conference it was clear that the referendum plan was in trouble. Many in Labour found themselves torn between respecting their manifesto commitment and enjoying the power that came with the massive majority FPTP had dealt them, and an anti-Jenkins campaign led by the AEEU union found much support. Tony Blair, although attracted to the idea of uniting the centre-left of British politics after nearly a century of division, did not appear convinced of the need for voting reform and had little stomach for leading his party where it did not want to go – on this issue at least. Jack Straw, as Home Secretary, put the project on ice in 1999 by saying that the introduction of new systems for Europe, Scotland, Wales and London should inform future discussions of the Westminster system and one should wait to assess that experience.

As the 2001 election approached, electoral reformers had their work cut out in preventing the whole reform project from being completely ditched. MVC even went as far as providing a major platform for Peter Mandelson, who was not pro-PR but who at least saw value in honouring an election pledge. The project survived – but only just. In its 2001 manifesto Labour accepted that the right way to change the voting system was through a referendum, but decided that it should wait to review the impact of the new voting systems that had been introduced in Scotland, Wales, Northern Ireland and London as well as for European Parliament elections.

To set the agenda for the government's review, the ERS proposed setting up its own review but, as the Society coming out in favour of reform would hardly have been newsworthy, it was persuaded that a more independent review would have more influence. Through MVC it was engineered so that the Constitution Unit would host the review and again the Rowntree Reform Trust provided the funding. It was not, however, a success. In striving for impartiality, it assembled a group with such opposing views that it was never going to be able to reach a view on the central question – should we have a referendum and if so on what? Its report in 2004[2] was a useful assembling of evidence but it did not produce any striking recommendations. Frustrated by the lack of progress,

2 http://www.ucl.ac.uk/constitution-unit/research/research-archive/tabs/
   archive-projects/icpr

the ERS was to produce its own 'Britain's Experience of Electoral Systems' in 2007.

As reformers awaited the elusive government review, the steam gradually seeped out of the movement. With no immediate prospect of a referendum, MVC lost its main source of funding and even found it difficult getting people to meetings to discuss an issue which was clearly off the agenda. The ERS could take consolation in a successful campaign to get STV introduced for Scottish local elections (the Scottish Parliament reached its decision in 2004 although the first STV elections were not held until 2007) and others could turn their attention to Lords reform.

The 2005 election provoked new interest in the campaign. The ERS described it as 'the worst election ever'. With only 35 per cent of the votes, Labour won a comfortable majority. Only a third of MPs won more than 50 per cent of the votes in their constituencies. The Conservatives were particularly badly hit by the bias FPTP can produce – in England they won more votes than Labour but Labour had 286 seats to their 194. The *Independent* led the outcry: in the days that followed the election their front pages blasted out the message that the result was unfair, that parliament was unrepresentative and that the government did not have legitimacy. But Labour, pleased at having a majority, was not listening – Lord Falconer, the Lord Chancellor, could only remark that:

I don't think there is a real groundswell for change.[3]

The Conservatives turned their attention to boundary reviews which they thought, erroneously, would solve their problems.

If there was a clamour, it was short-lived. Within a couple of weeks of the election it was no longer a story. In

3   http://www.guardian.co.uk/politics/2005/may/20/election2005.uk

January 2008 the Labour government finally did produce its review of electoral systems, a very good and fair-minded account, but it was ignored by the politicians and received next to no media attention.[4]

As the parliamentary term progressed, it was clear that politics was changing. In Labour the long-running feud between Blair and Brown was reaching boiling point, and although Labour rallied briefly when Brown first became Prime Minister in the summer of 2007, he was severely damaged by dithering over whether or not to call an election in the autumn. Moreover, in David Cameron he had a much more formidable opponent who would be harder to beat than Major, Hague, Duncan Smith or Howard. As the world economy went into crisis, with the autumn 2008 collapse of Lehman Brothers and emergency nationalisation of the banks, the foundations of Labour's rule crumbled. Although internationally Brown was hailed as the man who steered a way through, at home his past boasts of economic competence were coming back to haunt him. In moving towards the next election, the question was not could Labour win, but how badly would it lose.

These were depressing times for electoral reformers. If Labour were to call for a referendum on the voting system when it was heading for defeat, it would have been seen as a cynical attempt to save itself, and as a consequence would no doubt lead to the defeat of reform. If the Conservatives, however, were to gain an outright victory (which seemed likely for much of 2008 and 2009) any hope of electoral reform would disappear. The process that had started with such promise with Labour's manifesto commitment in 1997

4   *Review of Voting Systems: the experience of new voting systems in the United Kingdom since 1997.* Cm 7304, January 2008. Available at http://www. justice.gov.uk/publications/voting-systems-review.htm

had petered out. While there had been huge progress on other institutions, the reform programme for the Commons had ultimately resulted in a well-written but universally ignored government report that would live on only in the footnotes of others.

But then someone had a bright idea. And shortly after that, someone else had an interesting story for the *Daily Telegraph* about parliamentary expenses claims. Reform was back from the dead.

Labour's Deathbed Conversion 2009–10

Towards the end of 2008, Colin Hines got in touch with the Chief Executive of the ERS. Colin was a very experienced writer and campaigner on environmental issues – at the time he was playing a central role in launching the 'New Green Deal' which called on governments to respond to the economic crisis in an environmentally sensitive way. He was not too happy with Labour's rather patchy record on climate change, but his concern was that a Conservative government might be even less willing to get industry to clean up its act. Therefore his question to the ERS was: 'Can you guys not change the voting system to prevent this from happening?'

It had to be gently explained to Colin that electoral reform was not an easy business, and that in the prevailing political circumstances change seemed near impossible. But Colin, quite used to dealing with political impossibilities, was not easily going to take 'no' for an answer. However bad the situation might appear, the support of the environmental lobby was clearly important and the ERStherefore asked him to do what he could to get them on-side.

In spite of the political realities, Colin Hines's enthusiasm for one final push at the Labour government was such that in March 2009 a small private dinner was arranged to allow him to state his case. Those invited included Polly Toynbee who had so persistently called for reform in her *Guardian* columns, Neal Lawson of Compass who was perhaps the left's most prominent campaigner, John Grogan and Richard Burden as sympathetic Labour MPs, and others. There was general agreement that the task was a hopeless one, but when a few were left drinking coffee at the end of the evening, one of the company lamented we would never get a referendum before the coming general election, and if the Conservatives won we would not get one after it. Then added: 'But what if we went to a referendum on election day?' After a short silence as the apparent brilliance of the idea sank in, a new campaign was born.

If Gordon Brown was to be moved, the campaign would need strong support within the Labour Party. Soundings taken over the next few days found much enthusiasm. Progress, the more centrist movement of Labour activists, joined as well as Compass, and although the Fabians' constitution did not allow them to be formally part of the campaign, Sunder Katwala, their General Secretary, was supportive.

Thus a coalition was formed, powered by the staff and resources of the ERS but with the political muscle of its Labour-related partners. Willie Sullivan, about to become the Society's director in Scotland, was recruited to head it, and Blue State Digital, the internet campaigners who ran Obama's election campaign in the US, were engaged to run an e-campaign. It was not entirely successful, in that, like many other aspects of the Yes campaign, it took a concept that had worked for Obama in 2008 and tested it to destruction in the different circumstances of a low-temperature referendum in 2011.

The ERS's Council was broadly supportive, although tensions arose from time to time over the funding of a campaign over which it did not have complete control.

It was, however, the *Daily Telegraph* – never a friend of electoral reform – that allowed the campaign to really take off. In May 2009 it obtained and published details of MPs' expense claims. There was outcry. MPs had claimed for toilet seats, moat cleaning, a duck house (although that one was disallowed) and all sorts of things that ordinary people would expect to pay for with their salaries. Many had changed their designated main homes to allow them to claim more, some claimed mortgage payments when their loans had been paid off, and some are now behind bars for claims that were truly fraudulent. It emerged that MPs were no more honest that many in the private sector when it came to fiddling their expenses, but they did not have the tight rules to control their claims.

There always had been an argument that a better electoral system would make MPs more accountable, but here was concrete evidence of a lack of accountability. It was a godsend for electoral reformers. Getting the general public excited about the lack of fairness in the voting system had proved extremely difficult and talk of reform leading to a new form of politics was rather esoteric, but here was an issue which made the need for new politics understandable and over which there was real public anger. The level of anger and anti-political feeling (as reflected in the bizarre results of the European Parliament election in June 2009, when Labour came third behind UKIP and the BNP won two seats) was potentially dangerous, and there was a need to deflect it into a constructive channel.

Vote for a Change, as the campaign was now called,

exploited the mood to the full. Its most potent weapon was 'Gilbert the Gravy Train' – a miniature train designed for taking children along seaside promenades hired to take volunteers dressed as leading politicians around marginal constituencies and party conferences.[5]

The first breakthrough came at Labour's conference in Brighton in September 2009. In his conference speech Gordon Brown, taking most by surprise, promised that Labour's manifesto would contain a commitment to a referendum on AV. A noisy meeting of Compass, Progress and the Fabians followed that evening: while a few welcomed the movement by the Labour leader, most were angered by the inadequacy of his response.[6] Most, however, wanted a proportional system and not AV which many had previously dismissed as a hopelessly timid reform. A referendum on AV was an even smaller mouse than a commitment to legislate on AV. Moreover, when Labour was not expecting to win the election, what went into its manifesto was likely to be no more than something of historical interest. Even cabinet minister Ben Bradshaw announced at conference that he would continue the argument in cabinet meetings.

Vote for a Change, now stepping up the pressure, demanded a meeting with Brown – and they got it. Backed up by polling evidence, they argued that reform would be in Labour's interests in the short term (by showing openness to change) and probably for a longer period as well, but it was

5   I was not keen on this, as it verged on anti-politics and scapegoating. But I was prepared to accept it as exploiting and diverting a pre-existing nasty public mood for constructive purposes, rather than creating the negativity. In this, it was different from the use of the issue in the 2011 campaign or, for that matter, the distasteful targeting of individuals in the 2010 general election by some campaign groups (LB).

6   http://www.guardian.co.uk/commentisfree/2009/sep/29/gordon-brown-electoral-reform for instance.

clear that a polling-day referendum was not on the agenda. However, support from previous opponents of reform (such as Jack Straw and Tom Watson) as well as Brown, and sheer desperation, had made Labour more willing to give ground. What was offered was pre-election legislation for a post-election referendum. An incoming Conservative government could of course try to reverse the decision, but there would be political costs in doing so. At Brown's suggestion, Vote for a Change then took its arguments to Nick Clegg.

An anxious period now followed. At times nothing appeared to be happening, but eventually Brown got cabinet backing for his proposal, subject to the agreement of the Parliamentary Labour Party. When put to the PLP early in January 2010, it did not quite approve the idea, but neither did it veto it. The plan was now that the referendum legislation would be introduced as an amendment to the Constitutional Reform and Governance (CRAG) Bill that was already going through parliament.

In the weeks that followed, it appeared that the government was dragging its feet. The campaign understood that the problem was Ed Balls, one of the Prime Minister's closest colleagues, who was advising Brown to drop the proposal. Vote for a Change arranged a press conference in Ed Balls's constituency at which poster vans displaying the demand, 'Don't be a Block-Ed' would be unveiled, but when staff were already en route to Normanton for the event, ministers called Vote for a Change asking them to call it off as Gordon Brown would announce his plans in a major speech in a few days' time. The poster vans were garaged, and Brown did indeed make a public commitment.

But all was not over. By this time it was clear that the election would be on 5 May and parliamentary time was running out. On 9 February 2010 the Commons voted 365–187 for a referendum on AV. Labour MPs from the South and East were keen, hoping that it would help them with people wavering between Labour and Lib Dem, but many northern and Scottish Labour MPs voted for it on the assumption that it would never actually happen. The Bill still needed to get through the Lords, and the 'wash-up' process would decide which outstanding bills would be rushed through and which would not. In the end, time ran out for the referendum legislation.

Electoral reformers were furious. They felt betrayed. It appeared that all their work would come to nothing. Their only hope appeared to be a hung parliament, and they went as far as offering advice online to voters on how best to vote to achieve one.

As the election approached, however, the situation appeared to change. Following Nick Clegg's performances in the televised leaders' debates, support for the Liberal Democrats soared and an outright Conservative victory was no longer the certainty it once appeared. Reformers' thoughts therefore switched to how they would play their cards in the immediate aftermath of the election.

The ERS, Unlock Democracy and Power2010 (a campaign for constitutional reform that the Rowntree Reform Trust had run prior to the election) held several meetings and decided to unite under the banner 'Take back Parliament'. Billy Bragg, the singer and activist, contributed the idea of purple as the campaign colour.

The election result was something of a surprise. Predictably the Conservatives were the largest party, but they fell short of the overall majority for which they had hoped. The biggest surprise was that in spite of opinion polls, which at one point put the Liberal Democrats in the lead, many voters seem to have shied away from the party when they got to the polling booths. The Liberal Democrats only won 23 per cent of the vote and a mere fifty-seven seats – five fewer than in 2005. However, although they were profoundly disappointed, they still held a pivotal position in the new parliament.

Table: the May 2010 general election

	Votes	Votes %	Change on 2005 %	Seats	Seats %	Change on 2005
Conservatives	10,698,394	36.0	+3.8	306*	47.1	+97
Labour	8,609,527	29.0	-6.2	258	39.7	-91
Lib Dem	6,836,824	23.0	+1.0	57	8.8	-5
UKIP	919,546	3.1	+0.9	0	0	0
BNP	564,331	1.9	+1.2	0	0	0
SNP	491,386	1.7	+0.1	6	0.9	0
Green	285,616	1.0	-0.1	1	0.2	+1
Sinn Fein	171,942	0.6	-0.1	5	0.8	0
DUP	168,216	0.6	-0.3	8	1.2	-1
Plaid Cymru	165,394	0.6	-0.1	3	0.5	+1
SDLP	110,970	0.4	-0.1	3	0.5	0
UCUNF	102,361	0.3	-0.1	0	0	-1
APNI	42,762	0.1	0	1	0.2	+1
Turnout		65.1	+3.7			

*The election was postponed in one constituency, the safe Conservative seat of Thirsk & malton, so when parliament first met there were 305 Conservatives.

Seat comparison is with notional 2005 results adjusted for new boundaries.

Parties with either a seat or more than 100,000 votes are listed.

Candidates not affiliated to parties were elected in Buckingham (The Speaker Seeking Re-Election) and North Down (Lady Sylvia Hermon, Independent formerly Ulster Unionist Party). Respect and Independent Kidderminster Hospital and Health Concern both had an MP in the 2005–10 parliament but did not win a seat in 2010.

Shortly before election day, Take Back Parliament planned a rally in Trafalgar Square for the Saturday following the election, although with some apprehension – what if only a handful of people turned up? Their fears were not justified – around 1,000 protesters arrived, and they moved on to fill Smith Square where Liberal Democrat leaders were contemplating their options. Nick Clegg appeared on the steps and affirmed his commitment to electoral reform. For the moment, the future of electoral reform seemed to be in his hands, and safe.

Chapter 2

The Referendum Campaign

The Coalition Agreement and the Bill

The six days after 6 May 2010, when inter-party discussions on forming a government took place, were highly dramatic. Ironically, although the media seemed impatient and hysterical at times, the talks were pretty businesslike despite the high stakes. The events just showed that Britain's much-maligned politicians were capable of adapting quickly to a new situation. There is no reason to suppose that in future – whether under FPTP or a reformed system – the process will become any more disorderly. Quite the reverse. Politicians and the civil service have now experienced the situation once, lessons can be learned and the fairly impressive first try (since the last in 1895) to form a coalition outside war or national emergency set a good precedent.[7]

With hindsight, there were only three viable options given the election arithmetic: a minority Conservative government operating alone, a minority Conservative government with a 'confidence and supply' agreement with the Liberal Democrats or a coalition between the Conservatives and the Lib Dems. A Labour-led government would have been a

---

7   *United We Stand? Coalition government in the UK* (Institute for Government, 2011) analyses the process and points out that the UK transition was very fast by international comparison. See also 'insider' accounts such as those published by David Laws (*22 Days in May*, Biteback, 2010), Robert Wilson (*Five Days to Power*, Biteback, 2010) and Anthony Seldon & Guy Lodge (*Brown At 10*, Biteback, 2010).

very rickety enterprise. Labour and the Lib Dems together had 315 seats, and with support from the Scottish and Welsh nationalists, the SDLP, Green, Independent and Alliance the combined 'progressive' forces totalled 330. With the Speaker not voting and Sinn Fein not turning up, this would have given a majority of sixteen. Given that the SNP has a self-denying ordinance about not voting in what it considers England-only business, this would have fallen to ten. Night after night, such a government would have to corral Jeremy Corbyn, David Laws, Sylvia Hermon and David Blunkett into the same division lobby. It would never have worked, even in relatively placid times – let alone a period of some financial instability and the Lib Dems insisting on a new Labour leader.

However, much was unclear in the negotiation phase. Although Clegg had said the party with most seats should be given the first chance to form a government, he had not committed the Liberal Democrats to supporting the first-placed party and talks went backwards and forwards. Electoral reform was one of the key cards in this poker game.

Labour, it was to later emerge, suggested that a direct move to AV, without a referendum, followed by a referendum on something more proportional might be on offer, but a deal with Labour had problems. It would have been impossible for Labour's leaders to deliver electoral reform given the tight numbers and the near certainty that there would be enough anti-reform backbenchers willing to rebel and scupper the plan. There were many within the Labour Party who felt that the party had been defeated and should leave office with dignity rather than scrabble around. Some in the Lib Dems thought they should not prop up a defeated government.

However, Brown's willingness to talk about going so far

on electoral reform spooked the Conservatives, who then conceded some more ground to the Lib Dems. The result was the Conservative acceptance of a referendum on AV.

With hindsight, it is clear that a deal that committed the Conservatives to allowing a referendum, but left them open to campaign vigorously against it, and which split the two main parties of reformers (the Lib Dems and Labour) left the electoral reform project in a dangerous position. But these were days in which adrenalin was flowing in the nascent Yes campaign and nothing was going to slow its momentum.

It was notable that an AV referendum was a Labour policy, supported neither by the Lib Dems nor Conservatives, but it ended up being legislated by the coalition. This was not just a minor irony. The principal supporters of AV, in the Yes campaign and among the Liberal Democrats, were half-hearted in that they would have preferred a proportional system. A gift that kept on giving for the No campaign was Nick Clegg – not only because of his unpopularity at the time of the referendum, but also because of his eye-catching remark during the general election campaign that:

> AV is a baby step in the right direction – only because nothing can be worse than the status quo. If we want to change British politics once and for all, we have got to have a quite simple system in which everyone's votes count. We think AV-plus is a feasible way to proceed. At least it is proportional – and it retains a constituency link. The Labour Party assumes that changes to the electoral system are like crumbs for the Liberal Democrats from the Labour table. I am not going to settle for a **miserable little compromise** thrashed out by the Labour Party.[8]

---

8   *Independent*, 22 April 2010. http://www.independent.co.uk/news/uk/politics/i-want-to-push-this-all-the-way-declares-clegg-1950668.html (Emphasis added.)

AV remained a 'miserable little compromise' to its principal authors and advocates, and Clegg's hostile remarks about Labour read ironically now that hindsight suggests that the referendum was a poisoned crumb from the Tory table, much as Conservative MPs at the time disliked making this concession.[9]

Although the new coalition government was committed to a referendum, it was far from in the bag. The Conservatives had agreed to support the referendum proposal on the condition that it was part of a single Bill that would, as well as setting up the referendum, reduce the number of MPs and redraw constituency boundaries based exclusively on the number of registered electors in December 2010. This was a shabby deal if ever there was one. As Labour's John Denham put it, 'there is no philosophical, legal, practical or parliamentary reason for combining the referendum with boundary changes: it's simply that the changes favour the Tories.' Under FPTP, because of differential turnout and the way votes are distributed across constituencies, Labour gets more seats for its votes than the Conservatives, but rather than looking at the voting system, the Conservatives put their faith in adjusting constituency boundaries to correct this bias.

Moreover, any reduction in the number of MPs would disproportionately affect Scotland and Wales, areas of Labour strength where cutting seats would hurt Labour more. At no time was there any serious debate on what the ideal size of the Commons should be.

Labour's shadow cabinet, although firmly in favour of an AV referendum (although not all were ready to support AV), were deeply opposed to boundary changes. Inner city

9   Towards the end of the campaign, Clegg added the gloss that it was a 'miserable little compromise' only when it was offered by Labour and not in other circumstances. Not perhaps a good way to win over Labour waverers.

constituencies were generally smaller in size but often would have much higher numbers of people not on the register – the equalisation of constituency sizes should therefore take account of population and not just registered voters.[10]

In the Commons the Bill got a rough ride: it was not just the Labour side that objected but also many Conservative backbenchers who were opposed to the referendum concession that the Liberal Democrats had been offered. In the Lords, however, the debate dragged on for weeks before the government got its way. It was not until the last minute (17 February 2011) that the Bill was finally passed and the way was clear for a referendum on 5 May 2011 – the same day as the local elections.

The 'reduce and equalise' constituencies argument was not good news for the Yes campaign. Winning the referendum would need significant Labour support, but Labour's understandable opposition to the Bill introducing the referendum gave some the impression that Labour opposed the referendum itself. Some Liberal Democrats, such as Simon Hughes, were quick to allege Labour hypocrisy in opposing the Bill, an unfair charge which proved very unhelpful in building a common front of Lib Dem and Labour reformers.

The Yes Campaign

While politicians were engaged in debate, the two sides that would fight the referendum were preparing the ground and making their plans. Now that the referendum was a real possibility, there was a new challenge for organisations on the Yes side. The Vote for a Change campaign, which had

10 For reasoned objections to the 'reduce and equalise' policy see http://www.democraticaudit.com/boundary-changes

helped create the opportunity, had been about winning the argument at Westminster, but winning votes in a referendum was a different matter.

The organisation that would run the campaign had to be created. Discussions on how this would be done had started before the election and the main players eventually got together for a full day's meeting in July. There were two main blocks: the ERS, which had led the Vote for a Change Campaign, and the Rowntree Reform Trust with the Take Back Parliament coalition (which it had helped create) and Unlock Democracy (which it had funded). Although there were rivalries between the two, there were also close bonds of personal friendship which helped to achieve a consensus. By this time the ERS was looking for a new Chief Executive, and it was decided that the appointee would chair the campaign committee while John Sharkey, who had run election campaigns for the Liberal Democrats would be the executive head. Paul Sinclair, a media professional who had worked at Downing Street, was appointed Communications Director, and staff from the reform organisations were seconded to make up what became the 'Yes to Fairer Votes' team.

On the Yes side, a major concern was how the campaign would be financed. The Electoral Reform Society and the Rowntree Reform Trust had each pledged £1m, but this left them far short of what they calculated a national campaign would need. They (wrongly as it happened) expected to be outspent by the No campaign, but that they would have the advantage in the 'ground war' – people on the streets. Consequently they decided to put a lot of their resources into local campaigning, envisaging a general-election style campaign with telephone canvassing and traditional 'get-out-the-vote' (GOTV) activities. This, and it is a point we will return to later, was a fatal mistake. Certainly the Yes campaign had many committed supporters, but not nearly enough to contact the number of voters needed to secure victory.

Regional staff were appointed across the country, local support groups were formed (often with little active support), and yards upon yards of purple cloth were transformed into banners for street stalls and events that attracted limited publicity. There was a plan to reach three million voters by telephone canvassing and phone banks were set up, but volunteers were not forthcoming in the numbers that were needed and there were problems with the technology: in the end only 500,000 contacts were made, many of them not useful for GOTV purposes, and the project was abandoned. The ground war was not, of course, a complete failure, but small groups of people handing out leaflets in the main cities were never going to reach the number of electors needed to win. Moreover, local groups were often heavily reliant on Liberal Democrats who were frantically trying to defend seats in council elections, and the number of volunteers fell far short of expectations.

The Yes campaign also faced a difficulty in how to sell its product. Nick Clegg, after all, had described it as a 'miserable little compromise' and the Electoral Reform Society had dismissed it as a 'timid reform'. AV had been attacked by reformers who, understandably, had wanted something better, but now it was the only thing on offer and they felt they had to defend it. However, in December 2010, the No campaign was able to publicise past statements by Yes campaigners about AV, with pride of place of course for the 'miserable little compromise' but also the Electoral Reform Society's 126-year-old policy that AV was not suitable for electing a legislative body.[11]

11   As expressed, for instance, in my own *A Better Alternative?* (ERS, 2008) (LB)

Not wanting to get trapped into systems talk, Yes went for arguments about how AV would change politics, but it was stretching credulity. Admittedly the line that it was a 'small change that will make a big difference' was just about sustainable, but the claim that AV would 'make MPs work harder' was an anti-politics slogan that simply didn't wash – when No campaigners asked which MPs they wanted to work harder, there was no answer. Similarly, that AV would 'stop MPs having jobs for life' was far-fetched – AV would reduce the number of safe seats a little, but not more than that. That AV would 'clean up politics' and Nick Clegg's assertion that if people want 'more duck houses' they should vote No[12] were equally unbelievable, In 2009, at the height of the expenses scandals, calling for a new form of politics, including a better voting system, made sense, but not in pre-referendum 2011. As Paddy Ashdown commented:

> We were offering a solution to a problem people simply did not recognise. Yes, some people were exercised over expenses, or did not like the state of British politics, but they did not see the connection with AV.[13]

There were also issues of political strategy that the Yes side had to address. It tried to present itself as a non-party campaign – a movement of the people wanting a better democracy rather than one fronted by politicians. It used its own spokespeople, principally Jonathan Bartley, and the occasional celebrity, but they had to contend with a media more interested in politicians and parties, and much of the time they gave the impression of reformers talking to

12 *The Telegraph*, 18 April 2011
13 *The Guardian*, 6 May 2011

themselves. The approach also posed the danger of sliding towards a position of general opposition to the political establishment (and many of its messages demonstrated that this indeed happened) with the risk of marginalising, or even alienating, the politicians whose support they would need.

Quite apart from these tactical considerations, questions have been asked about whether the Yes side had the people, management and structure to deliver an effective campaign. Not only were regional staff given little support (although some had experience of political campaigning), but the campaign headquarters was not always a happy place. There was dissatisfaction over the leadership's failure to act decisively, chops and changes of policy, and a lack of consultation with junior staff. We are not in a position to judge how serious these complaints were – in the heat of a campaign a balance must be struck between consultation and decisions by those in charge – but the extent of the dissatisfaction in what should have been an exhilarating place to work suggests something was badly wrong. Chapter 5 analyses the failure of the Yes campaign and its messaging in detail.

The idea of running a non-party, almost non-political campaign on an issue like the voting system that impinged so closely on party politics was always going to be a stretch. It proved even more so, because so many of the civil society organisations which had been vaguely (or actively) sympathetic to the campaign were covered by charities law and could not take an active part once the referendum campaign was underway. The No campaign took a well-aimed shot across the bows of the potential 'people's campaign' by references to the Charity Commission in December/January, and the Yes alliance was much smaller, more political and more metropolitan liberal-left than was originally intended. It was a clear indication that Yes had been naïve about some crucial aspects of winning a campaign, and that they faced effective and unsentimental opponents.

The No Campaign

Just as the Yes campaign relied heavily on the Liberal Democrats, the No campaign was Conservative at its core. Matthew Elliott, who was head of the Taxpayers' Alliance, a right-wing think tank/campaigning organisation, was recruited to head it over the summer, and started work in the autumn. The first task facing the campaign was how to deal with its ideological heterogeneity, and come to its internal 'coalition agreement' between the Conservative and Labour elements of the campaign. In the event, this was turned to an advantage because from the outset No was forced to be explicitly plural in the way it operated, while the default setting for Yes was a cosy liberal-left position.

The main role of funding the campaign was taken by the Conservative side. According to Elliott, they received '100 per cent help' from the Conservatives.[14] The party, particularly after February 2011, was a vital source of organisational and political support and pushed No campaign messages through its networks; its donors were largely drawn from the Conservatives' friends (forty-two out of fifty-three were also Conservative supporters). This reflected the priority the Tories gave to the referendum after February 2011. Before Christmas there were accounts of CCHQ deterring people from donating to the No campaign, and the No campaign even considered not applying to the Electoral Commission for designated status because they

14 *The Guardian*, 4 May 2011

feared not having the resources to engage in a full debate (rather as the Welsh No campaigners did in the March 2011 referendum). It was ironic that Tory donors ended up funding highly partisan Labour No material blasting the Liberal Democrats that helped Labour retake Clegg's home base of Sheffield in the local elections.

But the campaign organisation and approach was genuinely bipartisan, with Lord Grocott highly influential in persuading senior Labour figures like Margaret Beckett and John Prescott to come on board as patrons. The Conservative patrons were deliberately chosen to be appealing to swing voters – Ken Clarke and William Hague rather than John Redwood, for instance. When the list of patrons was published in November 2010, Yes supporters scoffed at an array of Labour 'dinosaurs' but ordinary Labour voters were inclined to think more respectfully of these former ministers. The No team always had in mind the need to win Labour votes, and used its Labour figures prominently. In terms of party political spokespeople, a signal was sent that despite what Ed Miliband et al might say, a No vote was in line with the traditions of the Labour Party. Yes failed to respond adequately by using their own senior statesmen, like Alan Johnson, enough or in time, continuing with the attempt to be a 'people's campaign' long after that dream had died.

The outcome of the referendum was always likely to depend on how Labour voters split and giving a prominent role to supportive Labour politicians would have seemed sensible, but it did not happen. Some feared that giving too much priority to chasing Labour voters would put off others, but risks of the campaign ever being seen as a Labour one were negligible. Even in this unlikely event, how many Liberal Democrats would have voted against AV just because some in Labour wanted it, and how many of those Conservatives already prepared to vote against their party's position would have changed sides? The No campaign was more confident in its approach: although Chris Huhne described it as 'Tory from top to toe',[15] it seemed to be able to give John Reid, David Blunkett and Margaret Beckett more prominence than the Yes side could for Alan Johnson, Ben Bradshaw and Tessa Jowell.

However, a Labour Yes was created with the freedom to campaign with more partisan messages, but it did not seem to have the resources to make it truly effective. The No side could pump out the message that Labour people should vote No because Clegg wanted Yes, but there was no comparable campaign arguing that Labour supporters should vote Yes because Cameron wanted No.

The Labour 'No to AV' campaign was a considerable force, better financed and much more effective than its Yes counterpart. Labour No, in the shape of former MPs Joan Ryan and Jane Kennedy, was highly effective at lobbying undecided individual Labour MPs over coffee at Westminster, racking up endorsements. By the middle of the campaign, full-page adverts appeared in the press listing the majority of Labour MPs opposing reform, as well as extensive lists of Labour councillors and peers who wanted to keep FPTP. Interventions from old Labour stalwarts, such as John Reid, Margaret Beckett and David Blunkett, standing on the side of Cameron and against the Labour leader, gained much more prominence than the support of shadow Cabinet members for the Yes side. The No campaign devoted their second broadcast mostly to Labour speakers, with David Cameron the only Tory to appear.

15 *Financial Times*, 4 May 2011

The No campaign fought a ground campaign, with stunts and a battlebus to engage the local media, but not to the same extent as their opponents. The No campaign understood that the referendum campaign would be an 'air war' fought at a national level. Their priorities were to get their messages across through the media and party political networks.

The No campaign was, however, a highly controversial one. Claims by the Yes side that they were defeated by lies and dirty tricks may have ignored the many shortcomings of their own campaign, and their own ethical lapses, but there was justification for their complaints. A main claim of the campaign was that AV would cost £250m, enough, for example, for 2,503 doctors or 8,107 nurses. This, of course, was nonsense. The figure included the cost of the referendum, which was going to happen whatever the outcome, as well as £130m for voting machines supposedly required to count elections under AV. There was no need, however, for voting machines and election administrators did not believe them to be necessary.

Eric Pickles argued that AV could lead to compulsory voting and that people would face £50 fines if they did not vote under AV, with No speakers claiming, quite falsely, that Australia had needed to introduce compulsory voting to force people to use AV. This was greeted with utter bemusement in Australia.[16] Baroness Warsi warned that AV would let in extremists, when AV is the system least likely to do so.

For the No campaign, winners could lose under AV and losers win – which is true if by 'winners' one means 'FPTP winners', but if changing the voting system did not produce different results what point would there be in change? There were arguments that with FPTP each elector got one vote, but

16 http://blogs.abc.net.au/antonygreen/2011/03/no-link-between-alternative-vote-and-compulsory-voting-in-australia.html

that with AV supporters of eliminated candidates got more than one vote as their votes transferred to other candidates. The Yes campaign did not respond effectively to this charge.

Perhaps their most telling argument was that of simplicity. Of course there is nothing difficult in voting under AV, but the No campaign's clever comparison of the two systems (see Figure 2.1 in the Appendix) was perhaps a killer. It was all the more effective because it was, for the AV referendum campaign, a fair shot: it merely repeated the Electoral Commission's definition of AV.

Financing the referendum campaign

The official returns from the campaigns to the Electoral Commission will probably be published in January 2012 and after that the accounts required by companies law will follow. Finance became an issue during the campaign, with the two sides trading accusations about secrecy and dependence on small numbers of donors. Both published interim lists of donors towards the end of the campaign and these were published in *The Guardian*'s 'Datablog'.[17] The lists were not quite comparable in that the Yes campaign list was complete but the No campaign statistics covered only the period since the referendum bill was enacted and the formal campaign began. There will also have been late donations that reached the accounts after the lists were compiled, but the No budget will have fallen at least £600,000 short of the total Yes budget, despite Yes's frequent claims of poverty.

The Yes campaign raised more money than the No campaign – it had £3,436,642 while No had £2,595,130, including the first stage of the campaigns' grant from

17 http://www.guardian.co.uk/news/datablog/2011/may/03/av-campaign -funding

the Electoral Commission, totalling £114,000 each.[18] However, 63 per cent of the Yes funding came from two sources, namely the ERS and the Rowntree Reform Trust, both of whom chipped in over a million. Other associated organisations in the sector (Unlock Democracy, Make Votes Count and the Andrew Wainwright Reform Trust) contributed around £20,000 each, and a fair amount of 'donations in kind', presumably staff and resources, from ERS and Unlock Democracy, which had no equivalent on the No side. The remaining large individual and corporate donors (£8,000 and over) accounted for £493,000, and small donations and donations in kind amounted to £278,069 and £330,119 respectively.

The No campaign was dependent on its funding from wealthy individuals and corporate donations, usually from interests close to the Conservative Party. The largest single donation by some distance was £400,000 from Peter Cruddas, founder of derivatives traders CMC Markets and (as of June 2011) co-treasurer of the Conservative Party. Large donations totalled £2,223,000, among which was £20,000 from the bankers to the Electoral Reform Society, Arbuthnot Banking Group. Small donations raised £248,130 and there was a single union donation (£10,000 from the GMB, although other unions made contributions in kind by distributing leaflets).

The gap in small donations between Yes and No is surprisingly small, given that Yes was supposed to be a people's campaign and No the arm of the establishment. Yes arguably had a bit of a dependency culture on its two large sponsors and failed to raise funds effectively – although it is fair to note that the liberal donors being tapped up by Yes were

18 The total available for claim was £380,000 each. Further instalments were not included in the *Guardian* figures which were published on 3 May 2011.

smaller and had less money than the wealthy Tory networks used by No. Some on the Yes mailing lists complained about the number and tone of 'begging letters' that went out.

The Yes campaign cannot blame defeat on being outspent by plutocrats. Thanks to the ERS and RRT, and the existence of the standing organisational structure of the ERS, if anything they had more resources than the No campaign, and certainly enough to run a decent national campaign. It must ask itself why its money was spent so ineffectively – the campaign centrally owes that at least to the people who contributed.

The political debate

Although the Yes campaign tried an anti-politics approach, not using politicians as its spokespeople, it was soon clear that the media, and probably the electors, were more interested in knowing where the politicians stood. This was a difficulty for the Yes team – their most enthusiastic and most committed supporters were Liberal Democrats, but too much Liberal Democrat support, especially if it involved Nick Clegg, would be the kiss of death, particularly for attracting Labour voters.

Ed Miliband, Ben Bradshaw (who chaired Labour Yes), John Denham, Alan Johnson (a committed PR supporter) and others were all prepared to support AV, but with their party split on the issue they appeared reluctant to go for it, all guns blazing. What Ed Miliband had to say could not be faulted – the problem was that he did not say it often and when he did he did not seem to get the coverage that John Reid did when campaigning alongside David Cameron.

Labour decided, somewhat to the irritation of Liberal Democrats, that Miliband should not share a platform with Clegg. This was probably logical, both because of Labour sensibilities and for winning votes for the campaign, but the tensions became the story rather than the message of the campaign. At the formal launch of the Yes campaign, Labour produced an impressive show with speakers including Alan Johnson, John Denham, Ben Bradshaw, Ken Livingstone, Oona King and Neil Kinnock alongside Miliband, and with them, Liberal Democrats Vince Cable, Shirley Williams, Charles Kennedy and Tim Farron, and Green MP Caroline Lucas. The first question from the media, however, was 'Where's Clegg?'[19]

When the coalition deal was struck it is alleged that Cameron promised not to go in boots and all for the No campaign. It had seemed possible in the early stages that Cameron might have mirrored Ed Miliband's position, in being clear which side he personally supported but not throwing the party machine into the referendum conflict. However, three months before the referendum the result was looking uncertain, and Cameron and his colleagues weighed in heavily. This followed considerable pressure from Conservative MPs and activists and lobbying from the No campaign. The Liberal Democrats were outraged, particularly when the No campaign issued a leaflet claiming that Clegg had broken his promises (admittedly true) and that 'the only vote that would count under AV would be Nick Clegg's'. Even some senior Conservatives felt Cameron should have intervened and stopped distribution of the leaflet,[20] but Cameron's response was that the Conservative Party and the No campaign were quite separate entities.

Leading Liberal Democrats counter-attacked. Paddy Ashdown complained about 'a deeply vicious

---

19 http://www.bbc.co.uk/news/uk-politics-12888126
20 *The Guardian*, 6 May 2011

campaign';[21] Simon Hughes described the No campaign as 'fundamentally fallacious' and one that would reduce trust in the Conservative Party;[22] and Vince Cable commented that the Conservatives had 'emerged as ruthless, calculating and thoroughly tribal'.[23] But the real fireworks came from Chris Huhne who, it is alleged, confronted Osborne over the Cabinet table, accusing him, and others, of 'unacceptable attacks' on Clegg and of lying over the costs of AV. Baroness Warsi was accused of running a 'Goebbels-like campaign' for suggesting the BNP would benefit from AV.[24]

Huhne was of course castigated by the right-wing press, particularly the tabloids, which dismissed his outbursts as positioning himself for a leadership contest should Clegg topple. Others claimed the attacks stemmed from a deep unease among leading Liberal Democrats over the conduct of the campaign – recognising the folly of an apolitical campaign they decided, but too late in the day, to fully enter the fray. The counter-attacks for a while worried the No campaign, because they were given a lot of media coverage late in the process – a *Guardian* or *Independent* Saturday story would give it enough momentum to affect the Sunday and Monday discussion. But in the end it probably didn't help Yes because it once again identified the Lib Dems as the leading Yes voice, repeated the No messaging and seemed like whingeing about the rough world of politics.

What amazed, and angered, many AV supporters was the response of the Yes campaign to Huhne's attacks.

---

21 *The Times*, 6 May 2011
22 *The Guardian*, 6 May 2011
23 Ibid. Conservatives and No campaigners responded by pointing out that Lib Dems are no strangers to using rough tactics in their own electoral interests.
24 *Sunday Times*, 1 May 2011

They were dismissed as unhelpful. The Yes campaign leadership felt that Huhne was making the campaign too much of a Liberal Democrat–Conservative contest at a time when they wanted to play down Liberal Democrat involvement, but to disown Huhne when he was making the headlines, and when he appeared to be taking the lead in standing up for AV, was a strange decision that left some wondering whether the Yes campaign had any backbone.

We must not, however, forget other parties. The SNP were not keen on the referendum: they had not been consulted on the date, which coincided with the Scottish Parliament elections, and they were still waiting for their referendum on devolution. Nevertheless, they firmly pledged their support. Caroline Lucas was supportive, but a lone Green voice, and although Nigel Farage was on side and could have been a useful counterweight to the Conservatives on the right, there was little attempt to use his help. Plaid Cymru seemed too busy with the referendum on the powers of the Welsh Assembly to take much notice.

In approaching the referendum, the Yes campaign therefore had support from Liberal Democrats, from leading Labour MPs and from the smaller parties. This could have been an advantage – the point that FPTP was supported by the leaders of only two significant parties, the Conservatives and the BNP, did not sink in. However, its only real champions were Liberal Democrats. That was never going to be a winning position.

Public opinion during the campaign

The polling trends in Figure 2.2 of the Appendix tell a simple and quite comprehensible story of how the AV referendum went. At first there was a wide but vague agreement that reform was a good idea, with a fairly large number of Don't Knows. David Cameron's intervention in strong support of a No vote in mid-February 2011 seems to have generated a big swing towards No, after which Yes and No ran more or less level until the middle of April. Then there was a large, and apparently accelerating, swing to No until the end of the campaign as Don't Knows made up their minds and some softer supporters of Yes (particularly on the Labour side) switched sides. Yes seems to have picked up next to no new support during the campaign.

Despite enthusiasm from those who supported it, the strategy was flawed, poor decisions were taken and implementation was weak. That, unfortunately, is not just our assessment but that of the electorate: a survey of how people viewed the campaigns gave a sorry picture:

Voter assessment of the campaigns (%)

	Yes	No
Campaign was effective	14	33
Campaign was ineffective	30	17
Did not notice the campaign	27	23

While the public opinion trends tell a dismal story for Yes, and this must reflect on the campaigns' approach to winning votes, Yes was up against something that is, in political science terms, nearly an iron law. The 'no change' position will nearly always gain ground as polling day approaches. People who tell pollsters that they don't know will tend to be unconvinced about the case for change, not very interested and inclined in the end to plump for the No side. Even voters who feel sympathetic to change will drift towards No as a case is articulated for the status quo, and fears of change and instability are activated – particularly if the campaign for change has no convincing story about what problem the change would solve. Before the 1975 referendum, there was a strong lead for pulling out of Europe but this was reversed in the actual result; support for devolution ebbed sharply in 1979 in Scotland and Wales, and in 2004 for the North East regional assembly. Anti-reform campaigns turned around initial support for PR in several Canadian referendums. In New Zealand a concerted No campaign made a close-run thing of what had seemed a settled popular will for reform in 1993; a Yes lead shrank from 70–30 to 54–46. There are a few exceptions, including interestingly several in a burst of optimism in 1997–98 (Scotland, Wales, London, Northern Ireland) and the March 2011 Welsh referendum.

A change proposition needs to go into the last phase of a referendum campaign with a secure lead of 20 per cent or more, or consistently 50 per cent of those eligible to vote, if it is to stand a decent chance of winning. In the light of this tendency of the referendum, it looks as if the referendum was lost on 18 February when Cameron put his weight behind a No vote.

The 'keep it simple' argument was the most powerful one for the No campaign. According to YouGov's election day research, 76 per cent of No voters believed that this argument was one of the strongest, with 59 per cent trotting out the belief that FPTP was 'tried and tested'. Crushingly for the Yes campaigners, two very suspect arguments came next as reasons for voting No – 33 per cent of No voters thought that FPTP means that each vote is counted once rather than several times, and 27 per cent that reform is a waste of public money.[25]

25 http://today.yougov.co.uk/sites/today.yougov.co.uk/files/electionday_av_0.pdf

Yes supporters were more scattered between different reasons for favouring AV in the referendum, a sign that the campaign messages had been less coherent, or less convincing, than those put out by the No campaign. Some laughter in the dark may be the response to the principal reason cited by Yes voters (54 per cent) – that AV will make the overall result of the election across Britain fairer. This is something which AV will not necessarily deliver. 'It will force MPs to work harder to win and then keep their seats' was runner up with 46 per cent. Forty-four per cent cited its requirement for a majority of the local vote.

Despite the convincing victory for FPTP in the vote, public opinion was more nuanced, and suggested that there were people who could be persuaded to support reform in the right circumstances. When asked which statement best reflected their view about FPTP, voters were equivocal:

	UK voters %	Yes voters %	No voters %
'It is an excellent system that we should definitely keep.'	12	3	17
'It's not perfect, but it's probably better than any other way of electing MPs.'	50	11	73
'It's not awful, but another system would probably be better.'	25	54	7
'It's a bad system we should definitely change.'	12	29	1
Don't know	2	3	2

Even with the structure of opinion in 2011, enthusiastic support for FPTP was rare among the electorate and outnumbered by people who favoured reform. The median opinion was a somewhat jaded one: that FPTP wasn't perfect but the alternatives were likely to be worse. In a less cautious public mood, and with reform represented by a better option and a better campaign, people taking this view might be persuaded to support electoral reform in future.

YouGov also asked what people would have done had there been an option for proportional representation on the ballot.

	UK voters %	Yes voters %	No voters %
Keep FPTP	46	4	71
Change to AV	11	28	0
Change to PR	28	49	14
Don't know	16	18	14

This, more than ever, illustrates AV's status as a 'miserable little compromise' or as David Pannick put it 'the unhappy and unwanted child of a temporary marriage of convenience'. It is third in terms of what the public want – and therefore by its own logic should arguably be eliminated and the decisive round should take place between FPTP and PR.

The next chapter examines the detail of where and how the votes were cast in the referendum – the national extent of No's victory, and the small crumbs of comfort for Yes from a few exceptional localities.

Chapter 3

The Dimensions of a Disaster

Where voted for (and against) AV?

	% Yes vote	% Turnout
Northern Ireland	43.7	55.8
London	39.5	35.3
Scotland	36.4	50.4
Wales	34.6	41.5
England (exc. London)	29.8	41.6
United Kingdom	32.1	42.0

Source: Electoral Commission, *Guardian* datablog

The overall result was a crushing defeat for the proposition of changing the voting system to AV. It was worse than two to one against, which was at the very lowest end of expectations. Defeat was nearly total, across all social categories and geographical areas. Of the 440 counting areas only ten voted Yes, and only another eleven came particularly near (with Yes votes of more than 45 per cent).[26]

Outside London there was not much difference between England's regions – three regions were a touch above 30 per cent for Yes (North West 30.2 per cent, South West 31.5 per cent, and Yorkshire/ Humber 31.3 per cent), and five slightly below (Eastern 29.0, East Midlands 28.7, North

---

26 In England, counting areas were local authorities; in Wales Assembly constituencies; in Scotland Scottish Parliament constituencies; and Northern Ireland counted as one unit.

East 28.1, South East 29.7, West Midlands 28.5). Even within London, there was a clear division between inner and outer. Inner London[27] was 48.3 per cent Yes, while Outer London was 33.9 per cent Yes – above the English average, but fairly marginally so.

It may appear initially that the strongest Yes areas were those with experience of alternative electoral systems – Northern Ireland uses STV for all its elections other than electing its MPs, London uses SV for the Mayor and Mixed Member Proportional (MMP) for the Assembly, Scotland has MMP for the Parliament and STV for local government, and Wales has MMP for the Assembly. In the rest of England, the only non-FPTP elections are for the European Parliament and, in a few areas, for directly elected Mayors. However, this may be somewhat spurious (with the probable exception of Northern Ireland), because, as outlined below, the pattern probably owes more to partisan geography (i.e. the low numbers of Conservatives in Scotland and Wales) and demographics (London being the largest and most cosmopolitan urban area).

The distribution of the vote by counting area in Figure 3.1 (see Appendix) shows a clear 'one-tailed' pattern: most counting areas produced a result pretty close to the national average but there were a number of outliers to the right of the chart, i.e. atypical areas where there were high Yes votes. A defeat of this scale and relatively even distribution of vote can lead to no other conclusion than the argument was decisively lost at a national level – even the more favourable regions still saw big No victories.

---

27 Census definition: Brent, City of London, Camden, Hackney, Hammersmith & Fulham, Haringey, Islington, Kensington & Chelsea, Lambeth, Lewisham, Newham, Southwark, Tower Hamlets, Wandsworth, Westminster

However, some useful information can be determined from variations in the voting pattern. Looking first at the areas where Yes managed to win illustrates the niche nature of the appeal of Yes voting by the end of the campaign.

Where Yes won	Yes vote %	Turnout %
Hackney	60.7	34.1
Glasgow Kelvin	58.8	40.5
Islington	56.9	35.7
Haringey	56.6	35.6
Lambeth	54.7	33.1
Cambridge	54.3	48.2
Oxford	54.1	39.0
Southwark	52.7	34.3
Camden	51.4	37.3
Edinburgh Central	51.4	55.4

Source: Electoral Commission, *Guardian* datablog

These areas were all of a type – highly educated, youthful, liberal and cosmopolitan areas. Except for Cambridge and Camden, none of them has had a significant Conservative vote in recent elections. Except for Oxford and Cambridge, all are inner city parts of big metropolitan areas. The author's somewhat cruel observation when the results were declared, that 'if you had a referendum on legalising cannabis, exactly the same areas would vote Yes', expresses the cultural distinctiveness of the places Yes won. Voting Yes was not the mainstream option.

In some of these areas, notably Camden and Hackney, local Conservative leaders were in favour of a Yes vote (Andrew Marshall and Andrew Boff respectively) – a sign of a distinct local political culture, but also giving a sense that it was an option for local Conservative activists and voters to support Yes, or at least not to feel that their party loyalty demanded a No vote.

There were another eleven counting areas with more than 45 per cent voting Yes, and these were of the same type as the areas voting Yes – urban, liberal, youthful, educated and cosmopolitan. Glasgow Maryhill & Springburn is on the face of it a bit different, although the area has become increasingly popular with students and sustains a significant Green vote.

Where Yes nearly won	Yes vote %	Turnout %
Edinburgh Southern	50.0	62.2
Edinburgh Northern & Leith	49.9	53.7
Brighton & Hove	49.9	45.2
Glasgow Southside	49.7	43.3
Lewisham	49.3	33.1
Glasgow Maryhill & Springburn	47.6	36.5
City of London	46.4	42.5
Tower Hamlets	45.8	28.9
Cardiff Central	45.7	37.4
Norwich	45.5	40.9
Brent	45.2	30.8

Source: Electoral Commission, *Guardian* datablog

The political colours of the areas with a Yes vote of more than 45 per cent were mostly Labour – not Labour strongholds (except Hackney) but places where local political competition tends to be between Labour and Lib Dem (Islington, Haringey, Oxford, Cambridge, Southwark etc), Labour and SNP or Labour and Green. The House of Commons Library research paper on the referendum noted that there was a clear inverse relationship among the London boroughs between the number of Conservative councillors and the Yes vote.[28]

It is notable that despite the Liberal Democrats being most strongly identified with the Yes cause, none of their strongholds (with the exception of Cambridge) voted Yes. A high Green vote appears more predictive of Yes success than Lib Dem voting. Outside the big cities, areas with Liberal Democrat MPs did not produce particularly good results for the Yes campaign. In the Scottish Parliament constituencies roughly corresponding to Westminster seats held by Lib Dems, the Yes vote was 36.7 per cent – not significantly different from the Scotland average. Outside England'sbig cities, local authorities roughly corresponding to Lib Dem seats[29] produced a Yes vote of 31.3 per cent, which is a couple of points above the average but not spectacular (and includes the exceptional result in Cambridge). In the big city authorities where Lib Dems have MPs,[30] things were rather better – 41.3 per cent for Yes – but there was still not much sign of an effect of Lib Dem organisation and local leadership as distinct from the social composition of the area. A few stronger than average Yes votes were recorded in Labour areas of Southern England:

---

28 House of Commons Library Research Paper 11/44, Chart 3.2

29 Bath & North East Somerset, Burnley, Cambridge, Colchester, Cornwall, Eastbourne, Eastleigh, Isles of Scilly, Lewes, Mendip, North Devon, North Dorset, North Norfolk, Northumberland, Norwich, Poole, Portsmouth, Redcar & Cleveland, Sefton, Solihull, South Gloucestershire, South Lakeland, South Somerset, Stockport, Taunton Deane, Torbay, Wiltshire.

30 Brent, Haringey, Kingston, Richmond, Southwark, Sutton, Birmingham, Bristol, Manchester, Sheffield.

	% Yes	
Oxford	54.1	Pro-reform Labour MP
Bristol	44.7	One pro-reform Labour MP, one Lib Dem, one anti-AV Labour, one Tory
Exeter	39.0	Pro-reform Labour MP
Reading	39.0	Two Conservative MPs
Slough	38.1	Pro-reform Labour MP
Southampton	37.0	Two pro-reform Labour MPs
Luton	31.4	Two anti-AV Labour MPs
Plymouth	28.9	Pro-reform Labour MP (and two Tories)

Local political leadership probably played a part in producing higher than usual Labour Yes votes in some of these areas, although it might also be noted that some of these places (plus Brighton) are demographically similar to those that were always likely to be Yes-inclined. Plymouth, notably, was worse than average and so were some other less 'London-like' Labour seats lost in 2005 or 2010 such as Gravesham, Dover and Waveney. Luton is an interesting test of the political leadership hypothesis – its low Yes vote for a multi-ethnic Labour town in Southern England (by contrast with Slough, whose MP Fiona McTaggart is strongly pro-reform) suggests that the anti-AV stance of its MPs did affect local views, either directly or through the level of Yes activity carried out by Labour supporters in the town.

This finding adds another dimension to the incredible strategic folly of the official Yes campaign (as opposed to Labour Yes) in playing the anti-politics, anti-MPs card, and allowing Labour No so much political and organisational space to succeed in lobbying Labour MPs. The difference, in these southern towns at least, between having a pro-reform

Labour MP and Tories or anti-AV Labour may have been as much as 6–8 percentage points (compare Luton with Slough, for instance).

Among the areas recording the very highest No votes, there are some commonalities in their demographic and social make-up and their political culture. It should be no surprise that the heaviest No votes were in a distinct sub-set of Conservative strongholds where income and education levels are comparatively low, and the population nearly entirely made up of white owner-occupiers: Broxbourne, Rochford and Castle Point. Some of the other areas with very high No votes were rural and small town areas with, again, little connection to university or metropolitan areas (South Holland, Boston, Fenland). The only Labour stronghold in the top fifty counting areas for No was Hartlepool.[31]

Interestingly, well represented in the very worst results for Yes were a number of traditionally two-party marginal towns, many of which saw parliamentary gains by the Conservatives from Labour in 2010 or 2005. Cannock Chase, Tamworth, North Warwickshire, North West Leicestershire, Basildon, Dudley and Great Yarmouth are examples of this pattern. These are perhaps more significant and damaging for the hopes of further electoral reform than the predictable lower-demographic Tory strongholds, because these are the voters who have the power over which party wins general elections. A resounding No in these areas suggests to Labour that electoral reform will not help much in its battle to regain these seats in future elections.

This should not be surprising, because these are the voters for whom First Past the Post works reasonably well.

31 Conversely, the only Conservative stronghold among the top 50 counting areas for Yes was the City of London.

The vast majority of voters in places like Tamworth or Great Yarmouth support Labour or the Conservatives, and are not particularly interested in other options. The idea that Labour and the Conservatives compete for the support of the swing voters, and take it in turns to represent the town and govern the country, is one that has appeal in marginal middle England. The MPs for these seats tend also to be hard-working local representatives. A system like AV can be seen as allowing the odds and ends parties, including the Lib Dems, UKIP, the Greens and the BNP, to have undue influence over the result.

Who voted for AV?

The polling organisation YouGov conducted an election-day survey on the AV referendum and the other elections on the same day, with a large enough sample size to permit some analysis. The table below shows some of the key findings.

		Yes %	No %
Westminster voting intention	Conservative	15	85
	Labour	47	53
	Lib Dem	78	22
Sex	Men	40	60
	Women	36	64
Age	18-24	51	49
	25-39	42	58
	40-59	38	62
	60+	31	69
Social class	ABC1	41	59
	C2DE	34	66

Source: YouGov http://today.yougov.co.uk/sites/today.yougov.co.uk/files/electionday_av_0.pdf

YouGov's final headline figures were, in contrast to its other polls on 5 May and unusually for a company that has a good record of correct final calls, somewhat adrift, showing 62 per cent No and 38 per cent Yes. With this in mind, the numbers are illustrative of the difference between social and political groups, but should always be tweaked to reflect the 6-point error in the overall poll.

In terms of politics, the outcome reflected the campaign – half the Labour Party plus nearly all the Conservatives amounts to a lot more voters than half the Labour Party plus nearly all the Lib Dems. Among the Labour Yes vote, it would be interesting to compare with actual votes in 2010, because Labour supporters in 2011 include a considerable proportion of the 2010 Lib Dem vote, see Figure 3.2 in the Appendix.

In terms of class combined with party, there are some interesting findings from the detail of the YouGov poll. The following table illustrates the dramatic distinction between working-class and middle-class Labour supporters in particular.

Yes vote by 2011 voting intention and class

	Conservative	Labour	Lib Dem	SNP/ PC	Other	Don't Know
ABC1	15	53	77	56*	45	54
C2DE	15	40	79*	25*	40	35

* Small sample sizes make these figures very approximate.

Social class seems to have been irrelevant among Conservatives and Liberal Democrats, whose parties had the strongest messages for No and Yes respectively, but made a difference among the rest of the electorate, including

Labour voters as well as Don't Knows and supporters of the smaller parties. The Yes campaign clearly failed to communicate effectively with working-class voters.

Labour voters in London and the South (although apparently not the East) were inclined to support AV; otherwise there was a fairly even pattern of voting among each party's supporters across all the regions.

There is a strong relationship between age and voting, with young voters being most supportive of Yes and older voters the strongest No group. This may be of some long-term encouragement for electoral reformers – if indeed another referendum is a long time off, a lot of the No voters will have departed for the great polling station in the sky and been replaced in the electorate by Yes voters. But some of the age split will be a life-cycle effect, in that most people become more small-c conservative as they grow older: today's 20-year-old, politicised and pro-change Yes voter may turn into a mild advocate of not shaking things up too much by the time she/he is forty in 2031.

Given the Yes campaign's techniques, it is not surprising that it did best among the young and middle-class leftists and had little impact elsewhere. Its best work was done on social media, internet virals and activism, all areas that are more the province of youth. But some of its silliest aspects like the focus on celebrity endorsements, its self-absorbed 'democracy sector' culture, its stunts and above all its trendier-than-thou smugness are all the sort of things that win votes from North London hipsters, plus a little vague sympathy among people who will never turn out to vote anyway, and put off the middle-aged provincials who make up the majority of the electorate.

Who voted at all?

Turnout was driven to a great extent by the simultaneous elections for other bodies, but perhaps less than was expected when the Bill was going through Parliament. Northern Ireland and Scotland had, as expected, the highest turnouts for the referendum because of the elections for the Assembly and Parliament. However, the Welsh and English turnout seemed to be around 40 per cent and variations were more about the demographics of the local area than whether other institutions were up for election. In the few parts of England outside London without local elections, turnout was only just below average (40.4 per cent rather than 41.6 per cent). In the end, this sort of differential turnout had no effect on the result at all. The actual Yes vote was 32.09 per cent. The Yes vote, if turnout had been equal in every counting district (and the Yes share of the vote was the same as in reality), would have been 32.12 per cent.

In London, where a particularly low turnout was expected, 35.3 per cent was a pleasant surprise. Inner city London in particular saw some surprisingly high turnout figures; in a few cases, turnout in the 2011 referendum (with no local elections) was higher than in the last ordinary set of London borough elections in 2006. This was the case in Islington, Lambeth and Southwark, and in the other Yes areas turnout was not much lower than in 2006.

An increase in turnout was also recorded in Kensington & Chelsea, Westminster and Wandsworth, where local elections are uncompetitive and the dominant party is the Conservatives, but which still have elements of urban small-l liberalism on the one hand and strong local Conservative organisations on the other.

	% Yes 2011	% Turnout 2011	% Turnout change 2006–11
Kensington & Chelsea	32.3	34.3	5.3
Wandsworth	39.2	37.0	2.9
Lambeth	54.7	33.1	2.7
Islington	56.9	35.7	2.6
Westminster	38.1	31.4	1.6
Southwark	52.7	34.3	0.6
Haringey	56.6	35.6	-0.2
Lewisham	49.4	33.1	-0.2
Camden	51.4	37.3	-0.2
Hackney	60.7	34.1	-0.3
Bromley	28.7	41.2	-0.8
Ealing	43.3	36.1	-1.6
Hammersmith & Fulham	40.9	37.7	-2.0
Kingston-upon-Thames	39.5	42.8	-2.4
Greenwich	39.2	33.2	-2.6
Enfield	34.0	35.3	-2.7
Barnet	35.2	38.9	-2.9
Merton	35.4	39.8	-3.1
Harrow	33.9	37.8	-3.6
Havering	22.7	35.9	-3.6
Waltham Forest	41.6	33.8	-4.0
Richmond-upon-Thames	40.9	47.1	-4.0
Hillingdon	29.3	34.0	-4.1
Croydon	33.0	35.8	-4.6
Bexley	23.5	37.4	-4.9
Hounslow	39.2	32.9	-4.9
Sutton	32.6	38.8	-5.0
Redbridge	32.5	32.9	-5.6

Brent	45.2	30.8	-6.5
Newham	43.7	27.2	-7.4
Barking & Dagenham	29.7	27.7	-10.6
Tower Hamlets	45.8	28.9	-11.8

Broadly, the people who voted in the referendum were the moderately political public – the sort of people who vote in local, GLA and Welsh Assembly elections but may sit out European Parliament elections.

This, again, should have been foreseen – it was never going to be realistic to expect much more than this. The campaign did at least arouse enough public interest to drive up turnout in areas where there were no local elections towards normal second-order election levels. The explanation for this is probably mostly the official machinery (poll cards, official information, referendum broadcasts), although activity by the referendum campaigns must have made a difference. The achievement of nearly a normal local government election turnout in inner London, and the relatively high Yes vote, almost certainly owes something to the 'ground campaign' prioritised by the Yes campaign.

Conclusion

The circumstances were adverse to begin with. A referendum is an unsuitable way of starting a public discussion on an issue, particularly one as technical as the Alternative Vote, and it is clear with hindsight that the timing of the vote was about as bad as it could have been. However, even given all these factors, the overwhelming nature of the vote speaks volumes about the ineffectiveness of the Yes campaign. By the end of the campaign, it had made the reforming vote a stereotype of itself, the domain of the metropolitan liberal middle classes – a potentially broad coalition had been whittled down to its hard core. The next two chapters look at how that happened.

Chapter 4

Why AV was Always Going to Lose the Referendum

The Yes campaign, despite enjoying some initially encouraging opinion polls, was always at a disadvantage. If defeat was not quite inevitable, Yes still needed some luck and a very good campaign to overturn the structural disadvantages it faced. It had neither.

It had all looked so different in summer 2010. There appeared to be several reasons for supporters of AV to be optimistic about the referendum result. Opinion polls had suggested for some time that voters were inclined to support changing the electoral system, and what polling was taking place that summer confirmed that there was a considerable lead for the Yes camp in the AV referendum. The dramatic gyrations of opinion during the general election campaign suggested that the electorate was open to new ideas and political change, and the proportion of votes cast outside the big two was at a record level. After the election, predictions that hung parliaments meant chaos and instability had been proved wrong by the well-conducted coalition talks and the emergence of a government with a clear programme. Furthermore, even if 'progressivism' was a busted flush, then a vaguer project of 'modernisation' including Cameron on the centre right could encompass an updating of the electoral system.

At this stage, it is worth remembering, the Tory right was

most disgruntled about the referendum deal, with murmurs of complaint from backbenchers led by Bernard Jenkin becoming more pronounced over the summer. It seemed, for a while, that things were stacking up in favour of Yes – the most passionate No voices were non-mainstream right-wing backbenchers and some ex-ministers from the Labour government that had just been heavily defeated in the general election. Reform was supported, to some degree, by all the Labour leadership contenders and by Nick Clegg, who had been such a strong influence on the 2010 campaign.

However, even then there were structural and environmental factors that were always going to undermine the superficially strong Yes position.

1. Intrinsic problems of electoral system change

It is not an easy matter to change the electoral system in an established democracy. Most of the time rethinking the electoral system is part of a bigger change in political arrangements such as a new constitution, independence or a revolution. The early 1990s saw the last big wave of change after the fall of communism in Central and Eastern Europe, and other democratising change in Africa (including South Africa); none of these countries, it may be noted, chose FPTP. Remove these dramatic circumstances, when everything is in flux, and the tendency in most countries is for an electoral system to be left in place.

There are a few countries where changing the electoral system is part of the political game – Italy and France have both seen their electoral systems changed for essentially partisan reasons in recent decades (Italy in 2005, France in 1986 and 1988). In some other places, there are fairly frequent minor changes to the electoral system involving adjusting thresholds, electoral formulae and so on, as in

Belgium and Israel. In many places, the fundamentals remain unaltered for very long periods. Most of Europe adopted PR in one form or another sometime around 1918 and has stuck with it throughout democratic political history ever since.

The Anglophone countries, because of their less dramatic constitutional histories, did not get rid of their FPTP systems in a similar wave of change, but there has been a slow trend towards fairer systems. Ireland and Malta adopted STV, and Australia went over to AV, at the same sort of time that the PR wave swept mainland Europe in the years just after 1918. The next steps came in the 1990s when South Africa and New Zealand both junked FPTP, in favour of list PR and MMP respectively. The electoral reform cause has revived in some parts of the United States, with preference voting introduced in several major cities in California and Minnesota. Even the UK has seen non-FPTP systems accompanying constitutional change in Scotland, Wales, Northern Ireland, London and local government – plus changing over to PR for the European Parliament.

However, there have been a number of failed reform programmes in established democracies as well as our AV referendum. The Canadian Law Commission's report has sat on the shelf and there have been some heart-breaking failures at a provincial level in Canada in Ontario, Prince Edward Island and most disappointingly of all in British Columbia.[32] PR was defeated in a vicious referendum battle in Cincinnati, Ohio in 2008. Israeli reform processes have repeatedly run into the ground. The New Zealand

32 A Citizen's Assembly was convened in British Columbia and, after a long deliberative process, recommended STV. Its recommendation was approved in a referendum by 58-42, but it was not enacted because the provincial government set an absurdly high threshold of 60 per cent to take effect.

government has reopened the issue and raised the possibility of reversing the change to proportional representation that took place in the 1990s.

Political scientists such as André Blais, Matthew Shugart and Adrian Blau have pointed to the difficulties in starting a serious process for electoral reform, let alone seeing it through to a conclusion involving a change of electoral system away from FPTP.[33] To achieve change, a number of circumstances have to come together, the principal one being a series of results in which a main party is cheated by the system or seems to be permanently shut out of power, and then winning with a commitment to starting a reform process. This description fits what happened in New Zealand (Labour won more votes but fewer seats than the National Party in 1978 and 1981), British Columbia and Britain in 1997 quite neatly. The electoral system needs to be kept in political focus by such perceived injustice affecting a major player.

To see it through to a conclusion seems usually to take a measure of public anger, even disgust, with the results produced by the current system – as in the citizen-initiated process in Italy in 1992 and the success of reform in New Zealand in 1992–96 amid discontent with elite-imposed neoliberalism.

2. Problems of referendums, and the AV question in particular
It is one of many ironies of the AV referendum, and of referendums in general, that the demand for them tends to come from advocates of change while the mechanism is systematically biased towards producing an answer that upholds the status quo.

---

33 See for instance Shugart's blog www.fruitsandvotes.com, Blais's *To Keep or to Change First Past the Post?* (Oxford University Press, 2008) and Blau's chapter therein.

Referendums tend most often to lead to change when the issue being discussed is already well understood by the electorate, and an informed and considered decision is being made. In many cases, the referendum merely ratifies what has already become a consensus position (as with Scotland in 1997 and Wales in 2011). When a decision comes up as a surprise and the issue is not a familiar one to the electorate, the electorate tends to view the case for change as not proven and therefore vote No.

In the history of referendums in Britain, the question of Europe had been of high interest among the political class since at least 1961, the subject of extended public discussion and debate since 1971, and enshrined in law since 1972, before the referendum took place in 1975. Scottish devolution had forced its way onto the agenda with the Hamilton by-election in late 1967 and been at the forefront of public discussion from 1974 onwards before the vote in 1979. Devolution had been at the centre of a groundswell of political and civic discussion in Scotland again from 1988 onwards, another long lead-in to a referendum vote in 1997. Northern Ireland constitutional arrangements have been the primary issue in the politics of the province since the late 1960s, at least until very recently.

The referendums that have failed to produce change have been those where electors have not seen the point of the change, and the issue is unfamiliar – Welsh devolution in 1979 (and to some degree in 1997), regional government in England outside London, or electoral reform.

Referendums are at their worst in deciding issues of minority rights and issues that the public in general do not care about or understand.

›   Referendums are a majoritarian device. They are
    unsuitable for dealing with questions of minority rights
    and can be used as a means of majorities oppressing
    minorities (such as the Proposition 8 vote on gay
    weddings in California in 2008, the Swiss referendum
    on minarets in 2010, and numerous other cases).
›   A referendum campaign on an issue that the public has
    not previously regarded as an important matter, or even
    previously understood, is going to be unedifying and
    unlikely to be fought on the issue which is supposed to
    be the question. It also means that there is not going to
    be a mass mobilisation on either side of the campaign.
›   A referendum campaign in which there is no clear answer
    to the questions 'why are we having this referendum,
    and what problem would a Yes vote solve?' is going to
    be likely to activate the electorate's fear of change and
    irritation with those calling for the change.

The AV referendum fulfilled all these criteria.

Electoral systems have a minority rights component
to them, in that an electoral system may suit the interests
of an entrenched majority but still be unfair. At its worst,
FPTP can be a collusive arrangement between two blocs
of 30 per cent of the public to exclude the other 40 per
cent from any power or influence – but in that scenario, it
could still win a referendum 60–40. Although voting for
the two larger parties has fallen from over 90 per cent of
the vote in the 1950s to below 70 per cent now, this still
makes up a majority. Members of that majority will not
necessarily be sympathetic to the demands of their fellow
citizens who are less well served by the system. The plight
of the tactical voter under FPTP is always a minority one:

surveys are ambiguous but have found that only 10–15 per cent of voters use tactical criteria, and the rest vote for the party or candidate they actually want. This helps explain why the 'keep it simple' argument resonated so strongly in the AV referendum and the case for preferential voting did not communicate effectively.

Countries with written constitutions enshrining equality, minority rights and the power of the individual citizen can end up directly or indirectly creating a constitutional guarantee of proportional electoral systems; perhaps a written constitution and judicial intervention may be the route by which electoral reform eventually comes.

Electoral reform has long been a subject on which public attitudes are vague and ill-formed. There may appear to be a general consensus (about 60–30) in favour of a system that relates seats in Parliament more directly to votes cast, but asking the question in another form of words will tend to produce support for single party majority government. There is very little understanding out there about how exactly FPTP works, let alone the principles or mechanics of any of the alternatives. This made it fairly easy for the No campaign to activate the inbuilt fear of change among the electorate.

Referendums are a suitable mechanism for deciding some questions. For instance, it is hard to see a better way of resolving core issues about whether a part of a country should become independent or not, as with the southern Sudan, Quebec, East Timor and perhaps eventually Scotland. However, this is not universal even in peaceful separations in recent history, with the separation of the Czech and Slovak republics in 1993 taking place as a result of election outcomes rather than a referendum. But in general, some expression of full, informed consent is necessary to do something as basic as to break up a sovereign state. The argument that membership or otherwise of the European Union is a suitable subject for a referendum is also strong, given that it does involve questions of sovereignty – but this does not extend to every minor change in the frontier between the competences of the EU and the nation state (just as changes like the Government of Wales Act 2006 and Scotland Bill 2011 can take place without a referendum).

Referendums often just entrench a position that is already settled one way or another; the same result would have arrived if the question had just been legislated, but the referendum locks it in (although the practicalities of rescinding devolution, pulling out of the EU or scrapping the London mayoralty would all have been daunting anyway). The prize of a Yes vote was that it would entrench the new system, but the risk – a huge risk, given the conservative history of the referendum – was that it would instead throw up a new barrier to electoral reform and prevent a government from simply legislating it in future.

Until 2011, Chris Huhne's mooted solution of legislating AV but with a sunset clause requiring a future referendum to confirm it in place, following one or two elections in which the system was given a fair go, was feasible. Unfortunately, having held the referendum in 2011, this road is barred, at least as far as AV is concerned and probably for anything that goes any further than the rather feeble Supplementary Vote used for mayoral elections.

3. Timing: the political cycle
The timing of the referendum was up to the coalition negotiators and, at least initially, it seemed that the

Liberal Democrats had done well out of the deal. Several considerations suggested that May 2011 was not a bad date from the Yes point of view and it was a reasonable decision at the time for the Liberal Democrats. It seemed a good idea to get a big Liberal Democrat win enacted and implemented fairly quickly, to increase the party's eagerness about the coalition. Bearing in mind the uncertain conditions that prevailed in May 2010, a later date might have led to a fear (real or not) that the Conservatives would get what they wanted from the coalition and then go it alone without giving the Lib Dems their referendum.

Some opponents of AV (though not, significantly, the official No campaign) felt the timing was extremely helpful to the Yes side because the highest turnouts would be in the more pro-reform parts of the country – Scotland, Wales and Northern Ireland – because they would be having Parliament or Assembly elections. The fear, or hope, that differential turnout would favour Yes was always exaggerated, as London (also likely to be sympathetic to reform) had no other elections. As it happened, the turnout effect netted out almost exactly neutrally. A separate election date might have been better for Yes because there would be a lower turnout and voters would be drawn from two groups – people who cared strongly about the issue (probably Yes voters, particularly if an activist-led ground campaign actually worked) and people who always vote (probably older people with postal votes and likely to be No supporters).

In the event, May 2011 was terrible timing.

The Liberal Democrats, most associated with a Yes vote, bore the brunt of the government's loss of popularity during its first year while the Conservatives remained broadly where they had started; the Lib Dems collapsed from 23 per cent in the election (and significantly higher during the campaign) to around 10 per cent in voting intention. Their complicity in a Conservative economic policy they had argued against during the election, and the apparently casual reneging by Nick Clegg of a solemn, unconditional pledge on tuition fees, not only alienated their previous supporters but aroused huge hostility among Labour voters. In May 2010 the Lib Dems brought to the Yes side about a quarter of the voters and huge general goodwill; by May 2011 they only had a tenth of the voters supporting them, and the goodwill was replaced by scorn and contempt from Labour voters and grudging gratitude from the Conservatives.

The Lib Dems' slump has mostly been about politics. The Conservatives survived the first year in reasonable condition for several reasons. Parties newly elected to government are often slow to lose support from the people who voted for them – if not a honeymoon with public opinion as happened in 1997–99 there is often a reasonable period of happy marriage before things start going wrong. Conservative England also felt confident in its political narrative of events, and in Cameron's credibility as Prime Minister, and a sense has not developed that the government is incompetent. The passage of time will probably erode all these advantages, as will the reality of the harsh public spending settlement when it is reflected in cuts that affect people's lives. The sense of powerlessness and fear in the face of crashing financial markets and disorder in the streets that set in during summer 2011 may perhaps produce a mood for real change.

Calling the referendum for May 2011, as it happened

(and might have been foreseen), meant that the Yes party in the coalition was weakened and unable to connect with the electorate, and the No party was strong and confident. But it was the choice of the Liberal Democrats, not the Conservatives, to hold it then.

4. Timing: the local elections

The local elections may have raised turnout for the referendum, but the effect seems to have been fairly small and not very helpful. They also had a corrosive effect on the Yes campaign. Most (but not all) people who are interested in, and supportive of, electoral reform are in the Liberal Democrat, Labour, Green, SNP or Plaid Cymru parties, and also active in those parties. In terms of ground level activity, there was a conflict of loyalties that was usually resolved in favour of working for their party in the local or devolved election. The supply of activists devoted to the Yes campaign may have been greater if the vote had been taken away from the local election environment. The local election context also meant that the No campaign found it easier to get activists out to deliver its message. Conservative activists were engaged in local election campaigning and the party was encouraging (indeed, ordering) them to help deliver No leaflets as well. Labour activists fighting the Lib Dems in local elections also needed little encouragement to put out No leaflets bashing Clegg alongside Labour material. A referendum date away from the local elections would have made it harder for No to motivate people to go out and defend FPTP.

For Yes, the activist supply problem was severely compounded by the political context. Given the choice between working with Lib Dems in the Yes campaign or giving them a clobbering in the local elections, most Labour activists found the latter more appealing – particularly as hysterical Lib Dem leaflets about Labour's legacy started to appear. Taking the decision out of the context of local election competition would have enabled more local political unity for Yes in its stronger areas like Brighton & Hove, Manchester and Bristol. In 2011 there was particularly intense competition in several more otherwise fairly pro-Yes areas (Sheffield, Birmingham and Liverpool in particular) for the council (and in Edinburgh for Scottish Parliament seats). This was particularly destructive given that the Yes vote was concentrated in areas where Lib Dems, Labour and Green were in electoral competition. This may be one of the factors explaining why London (and Oxford) which had no local elections produced better results for Yes – more concentration on the issue and less heat from local political battles.

5. Link with the Conservatives' boundary changes

The nature of the Bill to implement the referendum was an unnecessary problem with which the coalition agreement saddled the Yes forces. It yoked together two basically different measures – one, relatively simple, to hold a referendum on AV and the other a complicated and contentious measure to reduce the number of MPs and rewrite the rules for drawing parliamentary boundaries. This was coalition management – each party got something it wanted, at the cost of something it had opposed before the election,[34] and the idea was to guarantee that both

---

34 The Liberal Democrats had already sold the pass on reducing the number of MPs. This had previously been a considered part of a package of reforms including a federal structure for the UK and proportional representation, but in 2010 they played a populist card and emphasised reducing numbers. They had previously been critical of the 'equalisation' argument.

sections went through. The alternative approach, of a simple referendum Bill that Labour could support even if there was a mass backbench Conservative rebellion, and a boundaries Bill that the Lib Dems would be whipped to support, was not tried. In fairness, it could not have been predicted at the outset quite how close and disciplined coalition unity would prove to be between May 2010 and April 2011, but by October 2010 it was clear that the format of the Bill was a problem.

The parliamentary struggle over the boundaries Bill weakened the nascent Yes forces. The boundaries Bill tainted the AV project for many Labour people, and the scorn with which Lib Dem ministers treated the arguments against the boundaries Bill (arguments which they had endorsed a few months previously) left a nasty taste in the mouth. It aroused the perennial Lib Dem distrust that Labour was not serious about electoral reform.

As a general rule of politics, following the 2010 election (and perhaps the election of Clegg in 2007), one can bear in mind that any development that *can* be interpreted in a way to poison relations between Lib Dem and Labour *will* be interpreted in that way. Two competing strategies were presented to Labour supporters. The Mandelson view was more or less: 'We've got to prise the Lib Dems away from being in coalition with the Tories. To do this, we should support them in the referendum. More hung Parliaments will give the left the opportunity to unite...' The Prescott view was: 'The Lib Dems are the enemy. They've shown their true colours by getting into bed with the Tories. We need a single-party Labour government, and this requires FPTP.' The Prescott line involved less cognitive dissonance for most Labour partisans.

6. The ambiguity of AV in the early stages of the Con–Lib coalition

Part of the problem with AV as such is that it has been seen as a 'progressive' political project for so long, and that the referendum was happening just at the moment where all those assumptions needed to be rethought. Throughout the campaign, the idea that AV was something to unite the 'progressive majority' was repeatedly raised.

This was a problem for getting a Conservative Yes argument off the ground – the Tory Yes forces always had to combat the perception that it was a fix designed to stop their party ever winning again. There were arguments in principle that Conservatives could support, and also a pragmatic case that it could lead to a long time in power for a Conservative-led coalition, but these were never really developed by the official Yes campaign.

This might have been affordable if a progressive majority really could be marshalled in favour of it. But the stale concept of progressivism could not cope with the fact that the Liberal Democrats were in government with the Conservatives, were operating a joint political strategy with the Tories and often echoing Tory rhetoric without any apparent reluctance.

Anything that required a sense of common purpose between Labour and the Lib Dems could hardly have been less likely to flourish than in the conditions of 2010–11. Labour's attraction to a system that looked as if it would give more power to Nick Clegg and those electors who were still supporting him was never going to be strong, in the circumstances.

AV in 2011 had a specific problem, in its ambiguity about which side of politics would benefit. In 2005, one could be fairly confident that it would help Labour; one cannot know what it would mean in 2015, but it is plausible that it would help the Conservatives. What polling evidence existed (thanks to *Channel 4 News* – it was a subject the Yes campaign tried to discuss exclusively with reference to pre-2010 evidence) suggested that it would indeed help the Tories in modern circumstances. Yes supporters tried to suggest that AV was inevitably in Labour's self-interest, but this insulted the intelligence of Labour commentators and voters – politics had obviously changed since the coalition was formed.

However, for politicians seeking to minimise unnecessary risks to their future prospects, Yes on AV would be a leap into the unknown. It is therefore not surprising that Labour's push for AV would be underpowered and that the Conservatives' Yes forces would not extend beyond their established small minority of reformers.

The logic of this position underlay the No campaign's success at lobbying the Conservatives to take sides and weigh in to the referendum campaign (although this is not to disregard its effectiveness – a bad No campaign might have failed to convert the opportunity into reality). There was a receptive audience for No arguments because of an understandable, rational concern. The same applied to many Labour people, relieved that the 2010 election had not been a massacre and optimistic that the party would win again under FPTP. Yes on AV would simply not deliver enough in exchange for the risk.

7. Labour division on the issue and the politics of being newly in opposition

Labour had gone into the 2010 election with a manifesto promising a referendum on AV.[35]

---

35 http://www.labour.org.uk/uploads/TheLabourPartyManifesto-2010.pdf p9:3

To ensure that every MP is supported by the majority of their constituents voting at each election, we will hold a referendum on introducing the Alternative Vote for elections to the House of Commons.

The promise of a referendum on AV is all that can be confidently deduced from this unclearly written paragraph,[36] but the language does imply the sympathy for a Yes vote which Gordon Brown had expressed in his conference speech in 2009 and afterwards. At no stage was the whole Labour Party committed to AV – it had been sprung on conference rather than going through the party's standard procedures. It was difficult for the party whips to persuade Labour MPs to vote even for a referendum in the vote on the Constitutional Reform and Governance (CRAG) bill in February 2010, and many northern and Scottish MPs voted for it on the expectation that it would never happen anyway, but it might win their southern colleagues a few votes in the general election.

Labour's support for an AV referendum in 2010 was therefore always a bit conditional and opportunistic, and in the very different circumstances after the election something of a hangover from the Brown era. Although Ed Miliband was convinced on principle about the merits of AV, he did not have a huge amount of political capital to spend within the party after a narrow and surprising win in the leadership election which itself took place using AV – which did not endear it to David's most passionate

36 On the face of it, the text is illogical and inaccurate. AV does not ensure that
    MPs are supported by a majority of those voting. Also, holding a referendum
    on the subject does not – as is very clear – mean that there is a Yes vote, so
    even if AV did ensure this, holding a referendum on its own would not. It has
    been suggested that the drafter of the manifesto went a little further than he
    should have done on AV.

supporters. It was not the sort of issue on which Labour would easily be led to a wholehearted position, especially on an issue it had not voted through conference and which was probably no longer in the party's (particularly the PLP's) interests.

In the circumstances within the Labour Party, and the broader political climate, Ed Miliband did more than the minimum to help the AV campaign, but it was never realistic to expect Labour to spend any of its nearly non-existent funds or prioritise AV anywhere near as high even as the English shire district elections, let alone Scotland or Wales.

Conclusion

These largely structural and environmental factors may be sufficient to explain quite how difficult the AV referendum was to win. There was not a lot that could be done about any of these problems once the referendum had become part of the coalition agreement. With hindsight, an AV referendum in May 2011 was a poison pill wrapped up in the coalition agreement for Lib Dems and reformers. But it was nowhere near so obvious at the time of the agreement, and the Conservatives' reluctance to concede it suggests that they had no idea it would work out this way.

They do not, however, explain why the margin of defeat was quite so resounding. For this, one needs to examine the nature of the campaign, in particular what might be called the 'unforced errors' of the Yes campaign. This is the subject of the next chapter, and it is not a pretty sight.

Chapter 5

Why Yes Lost Quite So Badly

It would take a sadist to find pleasure in examining the wreckage of the Yes campaign. The great majority of those involved, particularly at grass roots level, had their hearts in the right place, admirable ideals and enthusiasm for democracy and people power. The volunteers generally approached a difficult task with a positive spirit which is an uplifting contrast to the negativity, cynicism and manipulation of the No campaign. There was some brilliant creative work, particularly in new media, which was let down by the failure of the bread-and-butter work of the Yes campaign.

However, the strategy and leadership of the Yes campaign were not equal to the task. Perhaps nothing could have been, but the defeat was so much worse than it might have been because of the errors of the Yes campaign. This in turn casts a pall over the future of electoral reform; a 55–45 defeat would have kept the issue open, and even 60–40 might have been a foundation for something but 68–32 was a disaster. Those in charge of the Yes campaign must take a share of responsibility for the dark times in which a good cause finds itself. There have been a number of extremely thoughtful and constructive responses from individuals involved in the campaign, particularly Andy May (national manager of the regional staff of the campaign), Jessica Asato (Labour Yes) and James Graham (web and social media manager).

However, there seems not to have been much of an institutional response to the fiasco from organisations. Without learning, the next opportunity will be wasted as disastrously as this reforming moment has been. Lib Dem President Tim Farron was quoted in *The Guardian* (27 June 2011):

> Clearly we were not in total control of the Yes campaign, but it is clear lessons have to be learnt. A large amount of money looks like it was wasted and the whole thing has set back the cause of constitutional reform a long way.[37]

One hopes that this review will be candid, timely and published; Farron deserves credit for undertaking a task which others involved seem to have shirked. In the meantime, some thoughts are gathered here.

The fundamental flaw of the Yes campaign was self-delusion. It imagined itself at the head of a national popular movement and because 'group-think' set in early, it behaved as if this were true rather than a piece of wishful thinking. There was also sheer incompetence and wrong decisions separate from the movement delusion.

In fairness to the Yes campaign, there were decisions made by other actors that went against the Yes campaign. Among these, the most important was that of David Cameron, although some specific unforced errors by Nick Clegg, and the effectiveness of the No campaign, must also be mentioned. The decision about the wording of the referendum question was, in the event, unhelpful to the Yes campaign, although the Yes forces cannot complain about this because they did not submit any evidence to the Electoral Commission's consultation on the wording.[38]

---

37 http://www.guardian.co.uk/uk/2011/jun/27/libdem-av-vote-inquiry
38 http://www.electoralcommission.org.uk/__data/assets/pdf_file/0006/102696/ PVSC-Bill-QA-Report.pdf – see page 33.

The movement delusion

In her scathing (and very funny) post-mortem for *Liberal Vision*, Angela Harbutt hits the 'movement delusion' nail on the head:

> Ten hours after crushing defeat, the top item on the YES website was entitled 'Are you ready to make history?' It featured about a dozen hardened campaigners turning up in Trafalgar Square at 7am and unveiling a vast piece of purple bunting with the word Yes on it. The video went on to say 'We got *our* referendum and we say yes' (emphasis is mine). Note to wannabe communication professionals: if you use the first person possessive plural, make sure you aren't using it to describe a handful of hard core fanatics waving big pieces of fabric around at the crack of dawn.[39]

The Yes campaign ended up being as much about inspiring its volunteers as appealing to the public; its website frequently gave more prominence to pieces about how fun it was to volunteer for things, rather than arguments for voting Yes. Nasty as it was, the No campaign never lost sight of the consumers of the whole exercise: the voters. Yes was all about the producers; activism for its own sake. It was not the only point of comparison between Yes to AV and Labour's catastrophic general election campaign in 1983. If Tony Benn was ridiculed for claiming 1983 as a kind of victory for socialism because eight million people voted Labour, then Yes's residual self-satisfaction at six million votes and some 'activism' belongs in the same category.

The delusion of being a popular uprising rather than a difficult attempt to persuade 50 per cent of the voters

39 http://www.liberal-vision.org/2011/05/08/the-humiliation-of-the-yes-campaign/

plus one to support a small technical change in the electoral system had deep roots. There have been many wilderness years for the electoral reform movement and it was very tempting to feel that here at last was the promised land – and lose sight of quite how small the community of convinced reformers actually was. The referendum arose because of a successful campaign effort to convert a sudden tide of public anger over MPs' expenses in 2009 into a demand for lasting change. The referendum had been cemented in place after some spirited demonstrations of enthusiasm as the Liberal Democrats thrashed out the options for coalition. There was an idealistic belief in a new sort of politics, in which enthusiasm and activism can accomplish things, but wishing for it did not make it true.

From the 'movement delusion', all sorts of other errors followed.

› The prioritisation of the 'ground game' above other forms of campaigning, in a referendum which was going to be mostly a national 'air war'. A good activist network is nice to have, but to put one in place while neglecting mass communications like the freepost is ludicrous. Although there was effective use of the national media in the form of *The Guardian* and *Independent*, the Yes campaign failed to get its messages across to the papers that undecided voters might actually read. Some *Mirror* comment journalists were keen to get helpful, genuinely popular coverage of the case for Yes, and an article on page 2 of the *Mirror* reaches millions – but the propaganda war was not well fought.

› The campaign's descent into an attempt at rabble-rousing anti-political populism, and all the damage that was consequent on taking that approach.

› Trying to avoid using politicians in the campaign was a grave error (despite the qualities of the spokespeople the campaign used such as Jonathan Bartley); the media, and even the electorate, look to politicians to talk about politics. This led to cutting out not only mainstream politicians, but also mavericks such as Tony Benn and Nigel Farage who would have been good at communicating the idea of shaking up politics.

› A cringe-making search for 'non-political' voices, which led to an apparent obsession with celebrities.

› Failure to engage and give proper resources to the Yes campaigns within the political parties. A well-funded autonomous Labour Yes campaign from the outset could have achieved so much, and a Tory Yes campaign given proper respect and attention would have helped.

› An appearance of smugness and self-satisfaction which the 'democracy sector' in general needs to lose, rather than advertise to the electorate.

› Activists were often enthusiastic but badly briefed and not very knowledgeable about what AV actually meant.[40] The activist base was skewed towards idealistic middle-class young people, while mass communications in a national referendum requires the ability to talk to voters in language they understand. Voters start from a position of being sceptical about propaganda they are given by activists, and if that propaganda is unpersuasive and over-claims, the activism can end up counterproductive.

The failure of anti-politcs
The mainstay of the official Yes campaign was anti-political.

---

40 One neutral recalls that 'my unscientific sample on two street stalls resulted in wrong info each time: one explained SV, and the other didn't manage to explain anything more than it would make my MP work harder'.

It attempted to mobilise hostility towards politics and the political system. There were constant calls to 'Make Your MP Work Harder' and attempts to evoke the sour, angry spirit of the expenses crisis of 2009. This reached its nadir when the Yes campaign sent local and regional co-ordinators a jumble bag of toilet seats, rubber ducks, mock castles and the like. But even more juvenile follies were considered during the campaign. According to a campaigner quoted in *The Guardian*:

> We even brought in an advertising man to save us. He came up with the idea of constructing a giant pin-striped bottom to take around the country for people to throw things at as a way of illustrating that AV makes MPs work harder. It was desperate stuff.[41]

The first Yes referendum broadcast (in which 'voters' shouted at 'MPs' through a megaphone) was a piece of crude hectoring, complete with gross negativity about MPs and expenses clichés, which managed to be boring, incoherent, illogical and barely comprehensible while trying for populism.[42] While the second broadcast was a lot better (although it apparently focus-grouped badly), 'megaphone' illustrated a lot that was wrong with the Yes campaign.

Anti-politics was wrong for a number of reasons that should have been obvious at the time.

Pragmatic reasons
1. It would never have worked. The anti-politics of the Yes campaign was part of its 'movement' self-delusion, that the referendum would be won through some sort

41 http://www.guardian.co.uk/politics/2011/may/07/ed-miliband-nick-clegg-cameron
42 http://www.bbc.co.uk/news/uk-politics-13055101

of popular uprising against the political elites. This basically does not happen, except sometimes when the political system has visibly broken down and there is a general sense of crisis (as it did in Italy and a bit less spectacularly New Zealand in the early 1990s). While feeling in Britain at the height of the expenses crisis in 2009 was enough to ignite the process, the sense of passion was never going to last through to May 2011.

2. People who accept populist solutions to political problems, and regard all politicians with utter cynicism, are also apt to regard voting itself with cynicism and are therefore unlikely to turn out in a referendum. They are also likely to regard proffered solutions (like AV) with cynicism as well.

3. It insulted the intelligence of the voters, at least in the 'make your MP work harder' form. Voters could not see how AV could accomplish this, and they were right to be sceptical because the argument was indefensible. The weaker form of the argument, that many MPs would have to reach out beyond their core vote, was defensible but not particularly compelling, and the campaign slithered between the two forms of the argument, thereby looking devious. In 'megaphone' the defensible version was used first, but the narration then slid to the strong, indefensible version. All the populist rubbish of the campaign never matched up to the reality of what was offered.

4. 'Make your MP work harder' was probably the worst, least convincing form of words that could have conveyed this dubious argument. For a start, most people – even if they believe MPs as a breed are scoundrels – actually have a soft spot for their own

constituency MP and think they do a decent job. In the vast majority of constituencies, it is obvious that the MP is 'working hard', and a fair-minded person is likely to reject the suggestion that their MP is a work-shy freeloader. The unfair-minded voter, on the other hand, is not going to be impressed by this rather feeble suggestion, and responds instead with proposals of whips and scorpions.[43] The voter who took the view that MPs should work *a bit* harder would probably be happier with the Conservatives' reduction in the size of the Commons which would make MPs work on average 8.3 per cent harder.

5. It cut off the Yes campaign from support that could have been won from MPs themselves. MPs were understandably offended by campaign material that insinuated they were lazy or corrupt, and by the crude 'megaphone broadcast' put out by Yes. Some defected to the No camp. MPs' role was important in terms of opinion leaders, particularly within the Labour Party when many active members will have taken their cue from their MP (or former MP) as to whether to get involved in the campaign and how to vote. They could also be influencers in the local media, and introduce the ideas involved to local journalists and voters in a relevant and accessible way. The results analysis (Chapter 4) provides some evidence that the attitude of an MP could influence the local result significantly in some areas. It contributed to the willingness of Labour MPs to endorse the No campaign. 'We shot our messengers,' concluded Jessica Asato pithily.[44]

43 http://paperbackrioter.wordpress.com/2011/05/10/the-epic-av-referendum-post-mortem-blog-evil-triumphs-when-the-good-are-led-by-incompetent-halfwits/
44 http://www.totalpolitics.com/articles/158747/where-it-went-wrong-for-yes-to-av.thtml

6. It alienated potential allies. It was delusional to imagine that a campaign could do without politicians and traditional media. Many commentators otherwise highly sympathetic to reform, such as Polly Toynbee, had to dissociate themselves from the 'make your MP work harder' line of argument, often with words couched in a certain amount of contempt for the campaign. It alienated electoral systems experts who would otherwise have concentrated on the outright falsehoods of the No campaign, and encouraged an attitude of equivalence towards the dodgy tactics of Yes and No.

A *principled reason*

One can accept that principle takes a back seat to pragmatism in running a campaign; but principles should only be severely compromised when the promised rewards justify it. The Yes campaign fell between two stools – neither genuinely high-minded nor getting a decent price when it chose to sell out. The state of political discourse itself has been coarsened by the lies of the No campaign and the anti-politics of the Yes campaign.

Regard for politics is at a low ebb. For progressives and reformers, it is vital to have some sense of optimism and faith in the public realm; we must believe that politics and the political process can achieve something positive, and the main platform of Yes rhetoric contributed only damage to this objective. The best reason for not doing anti-politics is that it appeals to laziness, cynicism and synthetic populist anger – in other words, to the worst in people.

Incompetence

Much has been published online about the incompetence at the core of the Yes campaign, and the authors of those contributions are better informed than us to pronounce on the matter.[45] Clearly something went very badly wrong at the top, in message and management. The running of the campaign seems to have been extremely questionable, in terms of efficiency, decision-taking, management and basic financial control.

The culture of the campaign

Something was wrong at the heart of the campaign. Across the board, people who have written of their experiences with the campaign complain about bottlenecks in decision-taking, authoritarian diktats from the high command, secrecy, hierarchy and unnecessary factionalism. James Graham found that the culture of the campaign changed as the organisation coalesced in August 2010:

> The campaign suddenly, and at first imperceptibly, became rigidly hierarchical and obsessed with secrecy. I found myself in the odd position of being nominally in charge of the website while being excluded from talks with the contractors who were being charged with building the thing.[46]

Too much responsibility was loaded onto a small communications team (two full-timers for most of the campaign, compared to three full time, two part time, two researchers and two opposition research people on the No side), with the result that the structure created a bottleneck in decision-making at the centre. One insider put it:

---

45   Several of these are collected and linked via http://whywelostav.wordpress.com/
46   http://www.theliberati.net/quaequamblog/2011/05/07/crawling-from-the-wreckage/

The myth is that our comms team were draconian and amateurish. The truth is that they were woefully understaffed.[47]

The campaign also proved incapable of learning as it went on. According to Andy May:

Firstly, there were several full regional staff meetings where the staff were at the point of shouting that the phone banks were not working, the literature was inadequate, the messages weren't getting across and that the campaign was dysfunctional. Yet rather than address this and engage these people, most of the senior staff decided not even to show up to the final regional meeting four weeks out from the campaign.[48]

The point about the inadequacy of the literature is worth emphasising. Large quantities of leaflets were spewed out to local activists, some of whom were embarrassed by the quality of what they were expected to deliver. Some volunteers studiously avoided reading the leaflets, in case they were so alienated or depressed by the content that they lost their enthusiasm to deliver them.

A good organisation is more than the sum of its individual parts. The Yes campaign was less than the sum of its parts – some very creative and talented people were gathered for a good cause, but their efforts were refracted through a dysfunctional organisation. The hierarchical mentality described by Graham and others was the complete opposite of the doctrines of participation and pluralism that featured in the public utterances of the Yes campaign.

---

47 Private interview.
48 http://www.scribd.com/doc/55322336/Yes-to-Fairer-Votes-An-Insiders-View-published-on-Liberal-Conspiracy-http-bit-ly-lgw3Bk

Finance

There are clearly enormous concerns about fundraising and financial management within the Yes campaign; Andy May and others have raised these eloquently.[49] Disastrous and costly decisions were made about:

> › phone banking (the volunteer-based system ended up costing more per call than commissioning it commercially, and the data was mostly useless),
> › advertising,
> › a colossal unproductive investment in the ground campaign,
> › gimmicks, such as the dinosaurs sent out to journalists in November 2010

The lack of priority given to mass communications (the freepost and a central media operation with enough staff and resources to work properly) was scandalous.

A full reckoning must await the publication of the accounts required under election law (which are due between November 2011 and January 2012) and the accounts filed at Companies House (probably later in 2012), but it needs to be done for the future of electoral reform as a cause.

The Yes campaign was not outspent (despite its inferiority complex on funding). It made bad choices on how its money was used and for that it has nobody to blame but itself.

Flying blind

The research and polling strategy of the Yes campaign was <u>appallingly</u> implemented. There is little one can add to

49   Ibid.

James Graham's verdict, which is reproduced at length in the next two paragraphs.

> After the initial qualitative and quantitative analysis conducted over the summer, and a huge poll in November designed to help us identify what messages appealed to each demographic, opinion poll research effectively stopped and from that point onwards we were reliant on people's hunches to muddle us through. A frustrated research team found itself with nothing to do and was not empowered to work on its own initiative. Opposition research and proactive fact-checking simply ground to a halt.
>
> Research was not merely not commissioned; it was ignored. Our initial focus group work clearly showed that people were contemptuous of the idea that electoral reform would prevent corruption; people only approved of notions such as AV 'making MPs work harder' in the context of them having to reach out beyond their core party support during elections. Despite this advice, the campaign repeatedly sought to conflate the two. Similarly, the advice we got from veterans of the 2004 North East referendum was that celebrities were of limited value. Despite this, we ran a campaign that was obsessed not merely with celebrities but with ones who appealed only to the educated middle classes.[50]

Opposition research and negative campaigning against the other side is a vital part of running a campaign, and ignoring it is negligent, not high-minded. Negative messaging can work with the public, and attacks serve the valuable purpose of forcing the enemy onto the defensive and stopping them from developing a narrative.

50 *Liberator* #346 (June 2011)

The campaign was averse to supporting mock elections under AV, despite evidence that once people had used preferential voting they were inclined to accept that it was fairly simple and effective. However – and there is no getting around this, as it would be true in more than 90 per cent of constituencies were AV to have been used – the results would not be very interesting because there would usually be the same winner as under FPTP. The Yes campaign also gave the impression that it had something to hide, by neglecting to explain the details of how AV worked.

It is part of any campaign that knows what it is doing to monitor the public's response to its messages, and it is staggering that the Yes campaign failed to do this during the crucial period between the November polling (before the voters had started thinking much about it) and some late-stage focus-group work (when it was too late).

The freepost fiasco
The campaigns were each entitled to have a leaflet delivered through the Royal Mail, paid for out of public funds, to every household or individual voter.

In a climate where most of the government was hostile to the cause, and the press mostly either crudely hostile (in the case of the Tory tabloids) or bored and baffled by the whole issue (like most local and regional media), it was presumably particularly important for the Yes campaign to get its message across directly to the electors.

In the most baffling, staggering piece of incompetence of the entire campaign, the Yes campaign hardly used this opportunity.[51]

---

51 http://www.libdemvoice.org/?p=24502&utm_source=tweet&utm_medium=twitter&utm_campaign=twitter

> The Yes campaign sent out 8.6m freepost leaflets, at a cost to public funds of £1.5m.
> The No campaign sent out 40m freepost leaflets, at a cost to public funds of nearly £6.7m.

It was hypocritical of the No campaign to make the cost of the referendum such a central feature of their campaign while costing the taxpayer so much more than Yes. But in using the freepost they were only doing what any competent campaign would have done. The No campaign was also able to send a second leaflet to households where there was more than one person registered, allowing them to get more information over to multi-member households. They also, unlike Yes, did Welsh-speakers the courtesy of producing a Welsh-language leaflet.

The failure of Yes to use the freepost was not an oversight, but a deliberate, catastrophic error of judgement. It prioritised building up activist networks above communicating with the mass electorate, and for this decision alone it arguably deserved to lose. Part of the case against FPTP is that it depends on a small number of swing voters in marginal seats; the Yes campaign took this further and tried to swing a national referendum by precision-targeting a small sub-section of electors. They attempted to use ACORN demographic data to segment the electorate and identify key sectors for phone or direct mail, but the research was nowhere near enough to do this campaigning work properly. Neither campaign in the referendum had enough money to do it properly – to get the best from such an approach requires long-term commitment of large amounts of money, and an issue on which divisions of opinion are more fixed than they are over a low-temperature referendum issue. Polling was good for message testing, but useless for population segmenting or mass mailings.

To compound the problem, the Yes freepost is probably mostly remembered for an entirely unnecessary and incompetently handled racism row caused because the black poet Benjamin Zephaniah featured only in the London version of the leaflet and the Yes campaign had no convincing explanation of the affair, and their official Twitter voice completely lost its cool when challenged.[52]

Whingeing

There was an unfortunate tone to a lot of Yes campaign activity that can be summarised as 'snot fair'. It involved complaining to authorities such as the BBC governors, the Electoral Commission or the Advertising Standards Authority about news coverage or the – admittedly unpleasant and inaccurate – statements put out by the No campaign, or the sleazy insinuations made by George Osborne. Too much whingeing to the referee does not impress voters, who take it for granted that politicians are rude to and lie about each other. Nor does it give an impression of a campaign that is strong and confident in its arguments. The Yes campaign sometimes seemed paralysed by indecision about how to respond, with the outcome that it made no effective response at all. When the No campaign put out its – dodgy – costing of £250m, the Yes campaign did not manage to ignore it, or to knock it down effectively. It merely repeated the claim in trying to rebut it, a basic communications error.

---

52 http://wallblog.co.uk/2011/04/04/how-not-to-run-your-twitter-account-as-alternative-vote-campaign-rows-with-rivals/

The Question
The question on the referendum ballot paper was:

> At present, the UK uses the 'first past the post' system to elect MPs to the House of Commons. Should the 'alternative vote' system be used instead?

This represented an honest attempt by the Electoral Commission to write a fair question, but in detail it was not helpful to the Yes side. There are two points, in a relatively short question, which make reference to AV being a change and FPTP being the no-change option. Referendums in general tend to produce status quo answers anyway, but this form of words gave an explicit reminder that the no change option was FPTP. Without the contextual information, people may have considered the differing intrinsic merits of AV and FPTP as electoral systems, rather than a change/no change option.

It is another extraordinary failure that nobody from the Yes campaign or the ERS contributed to the Electoral Commission's consultation on question wording, while the No campaign, commentators on language clarity and electoral administrators did.[53] The argument might have been dismissed, but to fail to raise the issue of status quo language in the question was poor strategy. It may reflect another aspect of groupthink in the Yes campaign – that nobody could understand why the ordinary voter might feel more instinctive sympathy for 'no change' than 'change'.

The Conservatives
The most important cause of the weakness of the Yes campaign among the Conservatives was the unambiguous

---

53 http://www.electoralcommission.org.uk/elections/referendums/referendum

commitment of David Cameron to a No vote in his speech on 18 February. From this point on, the Tory Yes vote, apparently as high as 40 per cent in the Yes campaign's initial opinion polling research, bled away.[54] Cameron's intervention is visible in the graph of public opinion in Chapter 2 – it promptly closed the gap between Yes and No. It was a strategic victory of huge dimensions by the No campaign – having recruited a bipartisan set of speakers and patrons – that the referendum was framed in terms of partisan politics rather than being fought between two quasi-non-political campaigns.

As a new Prime Minister, in charge of a party whose voters feel positive about their government, Cameron had powers of charismatic leadership among considerable numbers of Conservative voters. Cameron's intervention also unlocked the network of Conservative donors to the No campaign and enabled No to dominate paid-for media and the 'air war' during the short campaign. The Conservative Party in its official communications pushed the case for a No vote, giving the impression that there was only one choice for proper loyal Conservatives in the referendum. Conservative activists were also a valuable distribution network for No leaflets.

Cameron's intervention contrasted with his previously lukewarm approach to the referendum, and was prompted by pressure from his party which was becoming restive at other coalition compromises and stoking itself into apocalyptic fantasies about what AV would mean for its future prospects.

It was something of a parting of the ways between two alternative political projects for the Conservatives in

---

54 It is extremely unlikely that this initial support from Conservatives could have survived a referendum campaign, even if Cameron had been less definite.

government. The road not chosen was a deepening of the coalition project into a liberal-conservative synthesis, which had been foreshadowed by talk among outriders such as Tory MP Nick Boles (though Boles himself was always a No supporter) of electoral pacts and continuing the coalition after the 2015 election. AV would have fitted very neatly into this framework, allowing controlled electoral competition between the two coalition parties which need not be very damaging because preferences would transfer between the coalition parties. AV enabled the existence of different but co-operative parties of the centre-right for many decades in Australia, and STV in Ireland also permits long-term co-operation between parties such as Fine Gael and Labour.

AV could have been the basis for a long period of centre-right hegemony – based on sharing and compromise, but also creating the possibility of a creative political synthesis. If there had been a mainstream Tory Yes campaign (Michael Gove was often discussed as a leader for this), it would have been based on this hope for the political future. Some of the less tribal Conservatives such as Steve Hilton and Oliver Letwin did not see the issue as all that important. A low-intensity referendum campaign, of the kind that some Liberal Democrats clearly thought they would get out of Cameron, would not strain the coalition in the short term.

What happened instead was an assertion of Conservatism, or more precisely the institutional interests of the Conservative Party. Rather than a fuzzy possibility of decades of power in partnership with the Lib Dems under AV, many Tories preferred the idea of a term or two of untrammelled Conservative government under FPTP,

and insisted that Cameron fight to preserve this prospect.[55]
Cameron threw his weight behind a No vote, rhetorically
and organisationally.

When Cameron made his choice (forced it may have been
by his party and the lobbying efforts of the No campaign),
the Yes campaign had two feasible responses.

> It could have redoubled efforts to put a Conservative
  face on the campaign, ensuring that at the very least
  someone right of centre was to the fore in most Yes
  activities, even if hopes of getting current Cabinet
  ministers on board had been dashed. There would have
  been enough peers, members of the London and Welsh
  assemblies, councillors and activists to give a blue veneer
  to the Yes campaign. While not a Conservative, Nigel
  Farage of UKIP would have helped too.

> It could have taken Cameron's move as a declaration
  of war and fought back. If No were prepared to permit
  slashing attacks on Nick Clegg under their banner, then
  Yes could dispense with any idea of being non-aligned
  and attack the Tories in order to win over Labour voters.

The Yes campaign did neither properly. Even after the
intervention of Cameron, polls shortly before the referendum
showed around 20 per cent of Conservative voters on the
Yes side, yet little was done to shore up support on the
political right. A 'Conservative Yes to AV' movement was

55 The Conservative story of the No campaign is written up at http://
conservativehome.blogs.com/avstory/2011/05/the-story-of-the-av-campaign.
html The argument for a Conservative Yes was a strong one; in the long term,
killing AV may have been one of the biggest strategic errors the British right
has made since resisting Irish Home Rule.

formed: although very small, it seems to have been crushed not so much by the Conservative Party's refusal to allow it a conference meeting as by the Yes campaign's failure to back it. It did not show Conservative Yes campaigners much respect or support; John Strafford was treated coldly when he mooted responding to Cameron's attack: 'If we went ahead with a press release, we were on our own... it occurred to me at this point that *Yes to Fairer Votes* did not really want Conservative involvement.'[56] Open-minded right of centre thinkers such as Phillip Blond were not cultivated, and Blond ended up drifting into the No campaign. Similarly, little attempt was made to look for support in UKIP, which had received nearly a million votes in 2010. Nor did Yes do a very good job of campaigning or even dog-whistling to the left. The Yes campaign of course had to consider whether going for votes on the right might alienate support on the left and vice versa, but it appears to have ended up going for neither with sufficient vigour – a symptom of its unrealistic approach of trying to de-politicise a campaign about something intrinsically political and partisan.

Labour
It may seem a basic element of campaign strategy that Labour voters were going to be decisive. Most Conservatives were probably always going to be No voters and the depleted number of Lib Dems would be voting Yes. The No campaign seemed to have a clear grasp of this. The Yes campaign, despite its generally poor cost control, cavilled and delayed when it came to funding Labour Yes.

---

56 http://www.opendemocracy.net/ourkingdom/john-e-strafford/
losing-av-referendum-personal-view-from-conservative-yes-campaign

Early neglect allowed the No campaign to steal a march on influencing and lobbying Labour opinion.

Jessica Asato of Labour Yes concluded after the referendum that:

> While the No campaign pumped out literature featuring Clegg across the north targeting Labour voters, Labour Yes had a small budget to print and hand deliver anti-Cameron leaflets in the areas where we had supportive MPs, which were mainly in the south. The only Labour voter targeted literature also had to be delivered by volunteers, while the mailed literature went to swing voters likely to turn out. The need to target Labour voters was realised too late in the campaign when the die had already set. Alan Johnson, Tessa Jowell, John Denham and other shadow Cabinet ministers did a fine job of trying to make the Labour case, but should have been used as the key spokespeople for the campaign from the start.[57]

Perhaps with hindsight, it would have been better for a Labour politician – maybe particularly a PR sceptic like Jack Straw – to have headed the campaign. It is revealing that Farron felt that the Lib Dems 'were not in total control of the Yes campaign': a back-handed admission that Yes was regarded as an arm's length Lib Dem campaign rather than a real cross-party effort.

Liberal Democrats in general, and Nick Clegg in particular, were poison among the undecided part of the referendum electorate. But they could not keep off the media and, in the context of the local and devolved elections of May 2011, it was unreasonable to expect them

---

57 http://www.totalpolitics.com/articles/158747/where-it-went-wrong-for-yes-to-av.thtml

to keep a low profile when they needed to fight for every seat. Nor could a campaign run mostly by Lib Dems grasp how deeply hostility to them ran within the Labour vote (for referendum purposes, the middle ground), including many people who voted Lib Dem in 2010 and felt betrayed. Clegg in particular seemed to put his ego before the needs of winning votes for Yes. The IPPR was one of the most sympathetic left of centre institutions to the Yes to AV campaign. It had done valuable intellectual spadework for the campaign in producing two reports during the long campaign, the first making an extremely convincing case against FPTP[58] and the second a nuanced argument for AV.[59] If there was any place where a thoughtful and bridge-building case could be made to Labour opinion about voting Yes, this was it. But Clegg – in an act of rudeness and ingratitude to his hosts as well as ineptitude if the aim was to win Yes votes – chose to devote a considerable part of his IPPR speech on 21 April to a strident partisan attack on Labour. He introduced wholly irrelevant and contentious attacks on economic matters. He also foreswore any further ambition to reform the electoral system after the AV referendum. While all his appearances lost the Yes campaign votes, this one was probably the most wounding and unnecessary.[60]

The No campaign knew what they were doing
The No campaign, although not without internal tensions and problems, did at least grasp campaign basics like targeting voters, getting its leaflets through people's doors, monitoring how its messages were going over, segmenting

58   http://labouryes.org.uk/ippr-report-calls-first-past-the-post-a-broken-system/
59   http://www.ippr.org/publications/55/1836/the-right-alternative?-assessing
     -the-case-for-the-alternative-vote
60   One of the authors (LB) seriously considered voting No at this point.

its appeal to supporters of the different parties and so on. It was not a particularly innovative campaign, but it was competent enough about the basics and that was enough to trounce the Yes forces.

The No campaign was not an edifying business: it went for emotion over logic in deplorable ad campaigns featuring helpless new-born babies and soldiers at the front, and even worse it could never stand up its claims about how much AV would cost. David Blunkett admitted:

> We are in the middle of an election campaign. People in elections use made-up figures. I have never used the £250m figure.[61]

George Osborne's smear of the Electoral Reform Society and the Yes campaign – a low attribution of financial self-interest – was wrong. A Press Complaints Commission ruling in July 2011 (too late to do any good) obliged *The Sun* to publish a retraction of its article reporting Osborne's false allegations,[62] but there has so far been no apology from the Chancellor.

In thinking about the campaign, one has to reflect that although there were dishonest claims made for a No vote, and hysterical support from the Tories and much of the media, the fact was that one side in the referendum were simply much better at campaigning in a national election than the other. It was unforgivable that it was the side that was less ideologically coherent, and had been called into existence for the campaign rather than existing for decades beforehand, that was better prepared and organised. The No campaign were Ryanair – charmless, efficient, populist

---

61 *The Times*, 5 May 2011

62 http://www.pcc.org.uk/news/index.html?article=NzIyMg==

– while Yes were Pan Am – a romantic history, perhaps, but unfortunately not flying anywhere.

No's core message was clear and focused, and the campaign knew where the votes up for grabs were. Accusations of being simplistic did not bother the No campaign because it was targeted on the ordinary non-political public and the campaign knew through focus group research that the arguments were working. The No campaign did not spend a fortune on opinion research – around £200,000 – but this was spread throughout the campaign period and was used constructively, for instance in message testing. The argument about wasting public money went over particularly well with working-class Labour voters, 37 per cent of whom felt it was one of the strongest No arguments (compared to 27 per cent across the board), and to some extent with voters who did not know which party they would vote for (31 per cent) – i.e. with the most persuadable electors.

While Yes was a picture of activist self-indulgence, No – and its establishment backers – kept it in check at least until after the result, when the self-congratulation of Dan Hodges in particular was hard to stomach.[63]

Peculiarly, although they had a well-established core message, in some ways the No campaign was more pluralist than the Yes campaign. It was better at speaking the right language to different audiences and even allowing contradictory cases to be made in support of a No vote. The No campaign supported a 'No to AV, Yes to PR' sub-campaign, on the model of the monarchists in the Australian republic referendum of 1999 who made a tactical alliance with people who wanted a directly rather than the

63 http://www.newstatesman.com/blogs/dan-hodges/2011/05/campaign -clegg-labour-cameron

indirectly elected President offered in the referendum. The Yes campaign on AV, by contrast, was paranoid about any implication that there was a further agenda beyond AV.

Conclusion

The great psephologist Sir David Butler commented amusingly about the tendency to heap up evidence to explain what happened so high that the result seems completely over-determined. A typical undergraduate essay on the 1945 election leads one to wonder why anyone voted Conservative at all – but in reality 40 per cent of people did. With the AV referendum, one probably *does* need a mountain of evidence to explain a 68–32 score line. Not all that went wrong is within the capacity of electoral reformers to fix, but it is the responsibility of those who care about the subject to work in a more realistic, competent and comradely way than we collectively did in the AV referendum of 2011.

Chapter 6

'Once in a Generation'?

Electoral reform will be back sooner than you think.

One of the more bizarre arguments deployed by the Yes campaign was that George Osborne, Chancellor of the Exchequer and one of the most hard-line advocates of a No vote, had said that the AV referendum would close down the reform argument 'for the foreseeable future'.[64] Therefore there was no point hoping for anything better than the system on offer, and all reformers should vote Yes. Echoing George Osborne is a bad habit, indulged in too many speeches from Liberal Democrat ministers, and this was not a persuasive argument to the undecided reformer. In any case, the 'foreseeable future' is a pretty short period, as a comparison of economic projections in June 2010 and July 2011 should confirm.

While one may have some fun with this particular claim, Osborne's comment was an example of a commonly held view among the Westminster elite, that the referendum in May 2011 would settle the issue for 'the foreseeable future', 'a generation' or even more floridly 'a lifetime'. The finality of the vote was common ground between Yes and No – each side had an interest in portraying this as a definitive contest, in the interests of short-term campaign priorities. Nick Clegg was towards the more extravagant end of the spectrum when he said on 21 April:

---

64 http://www.dailymail.co.uk/news/article-1376292/Chancellor-George-Osborne-calls-investigation-backers-conflict-interest.html

> We aren't going to enter into a Maoist, perpetual revolution...
> This is a once in a blue moon opportunity to change the
> electoral system. It's completely wrong to somehow suggest
> this is a stepping stone for something else.

When politicians talk about 'a generation' they actually mean
only about twenty years, but they wish to make it sound
longer; the incidence of blue moons is probably similar.

Arguments about future consequences are all conjecture,
but the 'finality' argument is a poor one. Even Lord John
Russell, in the 1837 speech in which he acquired the
nickname 'Finality Jack', did not rule out any further
progress on the franchise on the 1832 Reform Act – all
he said was that he felt personally bound by assurances
he had given in 1831–32. In the 1837 debate, Russell was
successful in seeing off the advanced ideas of Thomas
Wakley (MP for Finsbury in inner London) who favoured
further extension of the franchise, a shorter parliamentary
term and the secret ballot – but in the longer term Wakley's
ideas were too strong not to prevail (in 1867, 1872 and
1911 respectively). Nor was George Lansbury's defeat in
1912 when he called a by-election in his Bow & Bromley
constituency on the issue of votes for women the end of
that matter. Within six years (some) women were voting
in a general election; within ten, Lansbury reclaimed
his seat from the Mr Blair who defeated him in 1912,
and within twenty the struggle for franchise equality
was won.

Reform propositions sometimes emerge better and
stronger from initial defeat within a 'generation' (i.e.
twenty years or a bit sooner), as Scottish devolution did
between 1979 and 1997. This referendum is no more the
end of the struggle for real electoral reform than the 1979

referendums were for Scottish self-government or Welsh nationhood. That which is intended to be final often ends up temporary, and that which is intended to be temporary can often last for decades (like the interim House of Lords of 1911, and perhaps that of 1999 as well, and indeed FPTP in 1918).

FPTP remains deeply flawed

If one believes, as the authors do, that the cause of electoral reform in the UK is a sound one that is increasingly important given trends in society and politics, a defeat such as that of May 2011 cannot be the end of the road. The basic flaws with FPTP as an electoral system have not gone away, and are probably going to get worse as time goes on.

There are several trends that point to the re-emergence of electoral reform.

› **Low participation.** Turnout has fallen from a norm of around 75 per cent which prevailed from the late 1950s until the 1990s, to its present situation where turnout in an election perceived as dull (as with 2001 and 2005) is around 60 per cent and turnout in more interesting elections (like 2010) is around 65 per cent. Turnout is also highest among the older age groups, and as young people replace the old in the electorate it will probably continue to go down. While electoral reform is not a panacea for low turnout, and there are many complex factors that determine participation, it is evident that FPTP is failing to engage the public, and other countries that use PR systems tend to have higher turnout.
› **Low levels of support for elected governments.** The Labour government of 2005–10 rested on a particularly

shaky level of popular support, with 35 per cent of the vote in a 61 per cent turnout. In the 1970s questions were asked about whether the election of October 1974 (39 per cent of a 72 per cent turnout) was straining the frontiers of consent. The government that resulted from the 2010 election, although the parties that form it have a majority of votes cast, is based on Conservative policies supported by only 36 per cent of the votes cast in an election. How low does consent have to go before one concludes that the system is failing in its function of legitimising government? The current system offers a future of an ever-thinner basis of active consent for successive governments, perhaps worse than the 21–23 per cent of the electorate who determined the course of policy after the 2005 and 2010 elections.

› **Anti-politics and localism** could produce an appreciable number of MPs elected with no national agenda and with no need to form one. Their success might depend on communal identity, a local issue, a local party split, a newspaper campaign or the whim of a plutocrat. Electing an anti-political MP may be the only way in which some communities feel able to make their voices heard in a chaotic competition of single issue groups.

› **Strains between the different component nations of the UK** might well increase, exacerbated by the exaggerating effects of FPTP on representation. Labour-dominated Scotland and Wales (and the cities and the north of England) would be pitted against a Conservative-dominated south of England.

› **Protest and direct action** seem to be playing an increasing part in politics, particularly in regions and areas where people feel otherwise powerless and unrepresented and the state is losing authority and legitimacy. Powerful interest groups adversely affected by a policy will mobilise to resist it, usually successfully.

› **Sophisticated political tactics** may mean that politics becomes increasingly tailored to the interests of the small group of swing voters (and other groups such as older people who do vote) and ignoring long-term concerns and the interests of the nation as a whole. The concentration on 'Middle England' marginals dictated by the FPTP system is a hugely distorting factor in the terms of political debate, in that the outcomes are affected and that large swathes of the country (mainly areas where people already suffer from social exclusion) are marginalised in national politics. There is a postcode lottery in democratic power, but it is worse than that – the lottery is rigged.

Hung parliaments are likely

The arguments against FPTP remain valid. But what about the practicalities of a reforming moment?

John Curtice and others, notably the IPPR,[65] have demonstrated that FPTP is increasingly unlikely to achieve what its supporters claim for it, namely a decisive outcome to a general election, not that it has much of a track record of doing so anyway (1970 is the only 'clean' transfer of power from a working majority government of one party to a single-party government with a working majority in over a century).

Most of the explanation for the increasing likelihood of hung parliaments comes from two factors. One is that the number of MPs representing third and minor parties has steadily increased, as Northern Ireland politics has changed

65 http://www.ippr.org.uk/publicationsandreports/publication.asp?id=798

(1974), Scottish and Welsh nationalists have been elected in numbers (1974), and the Liberal Democrats have won more seats (since 1974 and particularly since 1997). In the electoral world of 1964, a 13-seat Labour lead over the Conservatives was sufficient to scrape an overall majority. In 2010, a 49-seat Conservative lead over Labour put us firmly in hung parliament territory. A main party now has to score a big win over its main rival in order to win a majority of seats.

Interestingly, even in late Victorian and Edwardian England the system made outright majorities hard to come by. The rise of the Irish Nationalists created a bloc of MPs not affiliated to either main party, and therefore various types of hung parliament in 1885, 1886, 1892 and twice in 1910. Three-party politics in Britain led to a couple more in 1923 and 1929. FPTP's ability to reliably manufacture majorities is confined to the Gladstone–Disraeli duopoly of 1868–85, the two-party state of 1931–74 (with wobbles in 1950 and 1964), and the period from 1979 to 2010 when first the Conservatives and then Labour had a dominant position in voting choices.[66] (See Figure 6.1 in the Appendix.)

FPTP is supposed to deter electors from choosing options other than the two main parties, and to prevent other parties being rewarded with enough seats to make a difference. It palpably fails to achieve either outcome.

The other factor making for an increasing likelihood of hung parliaments is the declining number of seats which are marginal between the two main parties when their national support is level. The more such marginals there are, the more sensitive the electoral system is to swings to either

---

66 One might add the 1895–1910 period when first the Unionists and then the Liberals had big victories and swings were large.

party – a small swing in votes is rewarded with a larger swing in seats which then exaggerates a lead in votes into a sufficient number of seats to constitute a parliamentary majority. At the height of the different two-party systems in the 1900s and 1950s this approximated the 'cube rule' – that a ratio of votes A:B produced a ratio of seats of $A^3:B^3$. In a parliament with 600 main party seats, this means that a 52:48 ratio of votes produces 336 seats for the winner and 264 for the loser, a moderate but workable majority. The ratio is now more like 1:1, so that in the example above the winner will have 312 seats and the loser 288 – which will mean a hung parliament if there are more than the token numbers of third-party MPs.

The reason for the decline in marginal seats can be found mostly in the trend towards regional polarisation in most elections since 1959; it is now a very atypical metropolitan English seat where the Conservatives are a viable proposition, and southern Labour seats are well off the demographic averages too. Differential turnout and the geographic distribution of votes have also led to a situation where the relationship of seats to votes is lopsided. A Labour lead of 3 percentage points in 2005 was sufficient for a comfortable majority, while Conservative leads of 7–8 per cent produced a narrow majority in 1992 and a hung parliament in 2010. In the 1950s there was a smaller systematic pro-Conservative bias.

Together, these two factors have created a situation where there is an apparently ever-widening band of election outcomes which do not lead to a parliamentary majority. In 1964 the difference between the pattern of votes that would produce a Conservative or Labour majority government was tiny; in 2010 it was vast.

In Figure 6.2 (see Appendix), the ranges of outcomes that produce hung parliaments on the electoral geography of elections since 1950 are illustrated. Assuming uniform swing, voting outcomes above the blue line would produce Conservative overall majorities, and below the red line would produce Labour majorities. Anything between the lines results in a hung parliament. As is apparent, there was not much of a window for hung parliament results in the 1950s when nearly all MPs were Conservative or Labour and there were more marginal seats, but the trend has been for the gap between the lines to widen steadily. There have not been as many hung parliaments as one might expect, given that 'hung parliament territory' occupies such a mainstream part of the spectrum of outcomes, because the Conservatives and then Labour piled up such large leads in 1979–2001. The 2005 election was a little different – Labour won a comfortable majority on a fairly slim lead in votes (comparable to October 1974) with the assistance of the pro-Labour bias of the electoral system. But in 2010 the sort of Conservative lead that produced a landslide in 1959, and a small majority in 1992, fell well inside the hung parliament zone.

Hung parliaments are likely to be the norm, rather than the exception, in the future, even if there is a partial reversion to two-party politics at the next general election. One can expect the proportion of Liberal Democrat MPs to fall, given political circumstances and boundary changes, but there will still almost certainly be more of them than in the 1980s, alongside just as many (or more) MPs of other parties. However, electoral trends so far since 2010 show a continued sharp regional polarisation and therefore, it is likely, fewer marginals than ever.

Hung parliaments, as we have seen, do not lead directly to electoral reform, but they do produce opportunities. In 1929 a hung parliament produced a Bill, passed by the Commons, introducing AV. In 1974, there was a vague hint of a Speaker's Conference but no more, and in 2010 it resulted in the referendum. Future hung parliaments are also likely to put pressure on the electoral system, for two main reasons. The first is that hung parliaments undermine the argument that FPTP produces strong single-party government, and a situation in which they become the norm rather than the exception would make it untenable. The second is that it provides leverage for smaller parties, particularly the Liberal Democrats, who favour reforming a system that mainly benefits the big two parties, and reform can be made a condition for co-operation or coalition. The leverage is strongest when the Lib Dems have enough MPs, and the gap between Labour and Conservative numbers is small enough, for them to have a genuine choice of coalition partner.

Conclusion
There will be another reforming moment.

The reforming moment in 1997, born out of Labour's constitutional radicalism and an underlying uncertainty about whether it would ever form a majority again, did produce results. Non-FPTP voting systems are no longer confined to Northern Ireland (Westminster politicians can always dismiss the province as a special case), but are familiar in Scotland, Wales, the European Parliament, London and mayoral elections. The Conservative–Lib Dem government's proposals for police commissioner elections involve SV rather than FPTP, and its proposed second chamber would be elected by PR. But the assault on the electoral system for the Commons was frustrated by Labour's increasing comfort with single-party majority power and the Whitehall mentality. It was renewed in 2009–11 but this time produced a counter-productive result because of the unfavourable environment and bad strategic choices. The struggle will be renewed, probably before very long.

The system is still broken – it is producing disproportional results, not much choice for voters, low participation, parliaments dominated by white middle-aged middle-class men and it is increasingly failing to produce stable government.

Preparation for a hung parliament should be a routine aspect of pre-election planning for all parties and the civil service, and electoral reform needs to be an aspect of that. Whatever the leadership now thinks, most Liberal Democrats remain passionate about reforming the electoral system. Members and MPs will exert pressure in future hung parliaments to put reform onto the party's own agenda and therefore into coalition talks. The other parties need to decide how to respond. What form this dialogue might take is the subject of the following chapters.

Chapter 7

The Art of the Possible

This chapter analyses the constraints on electoral reform which exist after the referendum, and some possible ways around them. It is intended to instil some realistic thinking about the environment that reformers face and raise some possible ways forward. While we come to some tentative conclusions in later chapters, this is intended to map out the possibilities without being too prescriptive about which is best; we are well aware that the 'best available' option will depend on the particular circumstances when a political space has opened up to permit reform.

There is a double lock on electoral reform for the House of Commons in present circumstances. To achieve the aim, unless there are other major constitutional changes, there needs to be an Act of Parliament (by legal necessity) and a Yes vote in a referendum (by what seems, unfortunately, to be established constitutional precedent).

The referendum constraint

One of the many unfortunate consequences of the 2011 referendum has been that it has now become effectively impossible to just legislate for electoral reform, even for a small change to the electoral system. If a precedent has been set for something as minor an alteration as AV to be put to a referendum, then any reform at all seems to qualify for a referendum.

It would have been better, in retrospect, not to have had

this referendum at all because it has closed off, at least in the medium term, so many options. It would be entirely fair for opponents of reform to cry foul if a future government attempted to legislate for AV, which was so resoundingly rejected in 2011, or for a system that resembled or went further than AV. It might just be possible to legislate for the SV, given it is such a small change, but a government would need a strong political will to do it and would probably have to offer a future confirmatory 'sale or return' referendum.

Referendum campaigns are a bad way of conducting a public discussion on most issues – the exceptions being questions of absolute fundamental importance which have already been extensively thought about by the public, such as EU membership in 1975 or Scottish devolution in 1997.

A future reform proposal needs to be more robust and capable of surviving a referendum campaign than AV proved to be in 2011. There are four possible routes to this.

› An **out-and-proud referendum on a radical change**. The Yes proposition would be for proportional representation for the House of Commons, be that by STV or MMP. In the AV referendum, the No campaign effectively campaigned against a caricature version of PR, rather than the reality of AV, and in a PR referendum it would do the same. The difference would be that the Yes campaign would be able to put a strong argument for the virtues of PR rather than a half-hearted argument for a half-hearted change.

› A referendum on a **package deal** including electoral reform and other constitutional change; in essence ratification of a new constitution. This would be the end stage of a longer process involving a constitutional convention or Citizens' Assembly. A constitutional convention followed by a referendum would be most likely to succeed if it were perceived as answering a new question and responding to a new situation. Scottish independence would necessitate a rethink of the constitutional arrangements in the remainder of the UK.

> A non-binding referendum on the **principle of change**. This would focus the debate on FPTP rather than an alternative, and probably maximise the Yes vote through uniting reformers (as they were not united in 2011) and doing less to activate the instinctive bias towards the status quo among the electorate. It would also set a process in motion, puncturing the complacent establishment assumption that reform will never happen, and with the right process (a Citizens' Assembly, probably) it could contribute to a more informed and considered case for change.

> Another **'modest proposal'** along the lines of the AV referendum. This could be AV itself, in a more favourable political context – or it could be another modest reform that is less vulnerable than AV to the rigours of a referendum campaign.

Each of these referendum options has its drawbacks. Reform is difficult, and option 1 ('out and proud') would arouse formidable forces in opposition, lose some of the more useful opinion leaders who were willing to support Yes on AV and face difficulty in persuading the public that it was the answer to a relevant question. Option 2 ('package deal') would probably only arise at a moment of crisis for the UK governmental system that had occurred for another reason. Option 3 ('general, non-binding') could probably win, but it would leave actually implementing reform until sometime in the future, and allow the process to be subverted or defeated even if there were a Yes vote. Option 4 ('modest proposal') suffers from the overwhelming nature of the defeat of AV in May 2011. Nevertheless, all are worthwhile possibilities.

The Westminster constraint

The House of Commons electoral system is unique in that it is decided by the people who themselves are elected under it. Everyone else has their electoral system decided by someone else – even in the case of the House of Lords, which does have a say on its replacement's system, the final decision is with the House of Commons.

An alternative system therefore has to be legislated, at least in the form of a referendum question, by MPs elected under FPTP. This is likely to produce a minimalist reform, as indeed it did in 2010–11, unless MPs are subject to overwhelming pressure or a strange conjunction of circumstances.

Getting a PR reform proposition through Parliament would be difficult even if the optimal circumstances of a Labour–Liberal Democrat coalition were to be in place in a future parliament. There would probably be a rebellion large enough to sink the proposal, because two groups within Labour would oppose it – supporters of FPTP and also the significant element (including Jack Straw, Ed Miliband and Peter Hain) who support AV as a better majoritarian system than FPTP.

Even if a PR referendum Bill passed, opponents would be likely to sabotage the details of its implementation, for instance by insisting on a turnout threshold, confusing the question or trying to insist on putting the least attractive form of PR they could on the ballot (such as closed-list PR).

The Westminster constraint indicates that a 'modest proposal' or some multi-stage procedure involving a commission of inquiry or Citizens' Assembly, is likely to be the most feasible scheme for achieving reform – unless there is a truly extraordinary conjunction of circumstances which makes 2009–10's expenses scandal, economic crash and hung parliament look like a blip.

Bypassing the constraints?

Given the severe limitations on the options and timing that the referendum and Westminster constraints impose on future electoral reform, it is reasonable to look to the possibility of getting round the constraints through institutional reforms.

There are a couple of possibilities for bypassing the referendum and Westminster constraints on electoral reform. One is the steady transfer of powers away from Westminster towards institutions that are elected by different electoral systems. This is already happening in Scotland and Wales, with the Welsh referendum of 2011, the Scotland Bill based on the Calman report, and the probability of a further shift in power undertaken by the majority SNP government in Scotland. Northern Ireland already has extensive devolution, and the longer peace and stability prevail the more autonomy it can take on. Although the House of Commons would remain elected under FPTP, its powers would wither away.

However, there is a big hole in the middle of the 'withering away' scenario – England. While a regional government was approved by an (unnecessary) referendum in 1998 in London, it was roundly defeated in the North East in 2004. The incoming government in 2010 has been cold about regionalism in general and has dismantled some of the structures that did exist. Regionalism does not have much leverage with public opinion – even in the regions with stronger identities, this does not necessarily mean that there is a desire for a tier of government. Localism is another possibility, although English local government is currently elected under FPTP, and the government's vision of 'localism' hardly seems likely to produce structures with the power and democratic legitimacy to be a serious diversion of power away from Westminster. An English Parliament elected under a non-FPTP system may end up in time being a feasible way of hollowing-out the FPTP concentration of power at Westminster. An English Parliament elected under FPTP would be a recipe for long-term Conservative domination. Historically, Labour has had a majority of English MPs in 1945–50, 1966–70 and 1997–2010; there would have been hung 'English Parliaments' in 1950–51 and 1974–79, and Conservative majority rule at all other times including the elections of 1964 and February 1974 which led to UK Labour governments.

Although in general we are dubious about 'direct democracy', this fashionable agenda could unblock the Westminster constraint, if not the referendum constraint. If the 'popular initiative' were introduced, electors would be entitled to put things directly onto the legislative agenda through a petition, provided that sufficient numbers signed. The exact mechanics could vary, but essentially a referendum would be required to validate the proposal. This could lead straight to a referendum on radical electoral reform – full-scale PR. While an activist network is not the most useful thing to have in terms of winning a referendum, assembling enough signatures for a petition is something that a well-organised reform campaign should find easy.

Although not as powerful, perhaps, the other sort of direct democratic proposition also has potential for pushing reform: the 'popular veto'. This means a referendum can be called by petition whose effect would be to invalidate a specific piece of legislation. In Italy in the early 1990s, the electoral law was repealed by this mechanism, compelling Parliament to legislate for an alternative system. Repeal of the constituency sections of the Parliamentary Voting System and Constituencies Act 2011, or to avoid all doubt the Representation of the People Act 1983, would amount to a veto of FPTP. Parliament would then be obliged to legislate for a replacement (presumably a 'modest proposal' type of reform like AV, SV or TR).

The other possible bypass route would be bicameralism. Supposing a government does succeed in reforming the House of Lords and introducing elections by proportional representation (STV or regional open lists), something has been achieved in modifying the winner-takes-all nature of FPTP. Already, since partial reform in 1999, the Lords has been more assertive and the lack of a party majority has meant that power has been more bargained than in the past (something the government intends to do away with through mass appointment of peers). An elected Lords, willing to use its powers (or, thinking more radically, with enhanced powers), would mean that governments would have to look further than a single party (or coalition) majority in the Commons to get its business through – there may even be explicit coalitions when there is a single-party majority in the Commons.

THE ART OF THE POSSIBLE

Of these bypassing reforms, the most immediately feasible is a second chamber elected by PR. This was the policy of all the main parties at the 2010 election and it is an active part of the coalition government's legislative agenda. It faces huge difficulties, not least in the existing House of Lords, but if implemented it would have a significant effect on softening the edges of the winner-takes-all FPTP House of Commons. The longer-term, dynamic consequences for the exercise and scrutiny of power, and for electoral systems elsewhere, might be profound.

Reform beyond the House of Commons

One long-term vision of the electoral reform process is that of an incoming tide. First came Northern Ireland in the 1970s, then Europe, Scotland, Wales, London and mayors in the 1990s, then local government in Scotland in the 2000s and (if the legislation gets through) police commissioners and members of the second chamber in the 2010s. Beyond this there might be Welsh and English local government in the later 2010s or early 2020s, leaving the House of Commons isolated and ridiculous as a continuing outpost of FPTP.

This seems a reasonable approach. The principal discussion points are the second chamber and local government.

How we elect MPs might be off the agenda at present, but Lords reform is another matter. How Lords, or whatever we decide to call them in the future, come to be Lords has been debated for a full century, but more intensively since Labour won in 1997 promising a more democratic second chamber. Progress, however, has been lamentably slow. Labour got rid of the hereditary peers, other than ninety-two

who were left as a temporary concession – ironically it is
only these remaining hereditary peers who are elected (by
the hereditaries themselves, using the Alternative Vote) –
but deciding what to do about the rest has been a much
trickier job.

In 1999 Labour gave us the Wakeham Commission
which rather timidly proposed that only a small proportion
should be elected. This was followed by a White Paper
in 2001 which did not move the debate much further
forwards. Then in 2003 Labour allowed a series of votes
on what percentage of the Lords should be elected: the
Commons voted against every option that was presented
amid scenes of procedural confusion. The vote for an 80
per cent elected chamber was lost 284–281, and it seems
possible that some MPs ended up in the wrong division
lobby because of confusion and the wearying effects of a
long evening in the bar. Predictably, every reform option
was resoundingly defeated in the Lords, who upheld the
idea of an appointed chamber.

The 2003 votes did not suggest a clear way forward
and the government's determination flagged. Tony Blair
decided he was not that keen on more powerful elected
institutions and with the departure of Robin Cook from
the government over Iraq, the reforming energy was lost.
Parties continued to talk, but without anyone regarding
it as an issue of sufficient importance to justify the
parliamentary time it would take up. If it had been taken
up, there would have been the long debates on the terms
of office, the different powers of the two chambers, the
transitional arrangements, the name of the chamber and so
on. The parties and parliament were growing accustomed
to the more assertive House of Lords that the banishment

of the hereditaries and the removal of the inbuilt Tory majority had created. Another government white paper proposing a half-elected, half-appointed second chamber appeared in 2007 but, when the Commons voted on it, two options were approved: a fully elected house was the clear winner, closely followed by 80 per cent elected. However, there were a few questions around the validity of the votes – some, it appeared, had voted for the furthest reaching reform knowing that it was never going to be implemented, while a compromise position might have stood a chance of success.

When it came to the 2010 general election, all three major parties again committed themselves to Lords reform, and in May 2011 a new Bill calling for an 80 per cent elected chamber was introduced. Some saw this as a consolation prize for Nick Clegg and the Liberal Democrats, still smarting over their defeat in the referendum. Whether this Bill will succeed where other initiatives have failed remains to be seen: the failure rate of Lords reform proposals is very high. Unfortunately it fell to Nick Clegg to introduce it. With Clegg's popularity near rock bottom, there appeared a danger that Lords reform would suffer the same fate as AV – whatever Clegg wanted, many, particularly in the Labour Party, would oppose.

For most electoral reformers, the campaign for Lords reform is a second-division match. It is the Commons that decides who is in government, and while the Lords can tinker with legislation and delay it, what happens in the Commons is much more important. Nevertheless, Lords reform may yet provide a useful opportunity to campaign for something better than FPTP. And a campaign for a proportional system is one with a realistic chance of success.

The arguments that are used against PR for the Commons do not apply when it comes to the Lords. There is broad cross-party agreement that no single party should dominate the Lords and arguments about the need for 'strong government' do not arise. Moreover, the Lords are already broadly proportional. And while MPs resist the competition in their constituencies which proportionality would provide, Lords do not have personal fiefdoms which they need to protect. From the point of view of acceptability among MPs, it is a positive advantage for Senators (whatever they may be called) not to have geographical constituencies so that there is not competition to be the voice of the local area.

The Liberal Democrats have long favoured STV for the Lords, but Labour has also advocated a proportional system – a semi-open-list system – and even in Conservative ranks support for FPTP has been half-hearted. Here, then, is a real opportunity.

The case for using STV for Lords elections is strong. If we are to have a second chamber which effectively scrutinises legislation we need a chamber of reasonably independent-minded people. We cannot take party politics out of the Lords and we should not try to do so: those concerned with public policy will have political views and will align themselves with one party or another. With STV, however, people vote for candidates and not for parties, and even if they choose to support candidates by party, they can still choose, for example, which Labour candidate they want to do the job. Having been elected with their own mandates, there is more chance they will feel able to question policy even when it means questioning their party leaders.

The prospects for STV for Lords elections got a boost in 2005 when a cross-party group of eminent MPs – the late

Robin Cook and Tony Wright for Labour, Ken Clarke and Sir George Younger of the Conservatives and Paul (now Lord) Tyler of the Liberal Democrats – produced a booklet arguing for a second chamber elected by STV. That Clarke and Younger are now government ministers demonstrates winning support for STV in Conservative ranks is far from impossible.

However, while STV has its uses in the Lords, one can also point to significant advantages of list-based PR systems in this context. If the second chamber is supposed to do something different from the Commons (a revising chamber with some claims to independence and expertise), there are arguments for an electoral system that produces a different type of personality and life experience among elected representatives. Candidate-centred systems depend on personal ambition and a long-term commitment to campaigning, which may not mix well with the role of the Lords/Senate. List electoral systems come in many varieties – while closed-list PR (as used in the European Parliament election) is obviously unsuitable for a second chamber, there is a legitimate discussion to be had about the alternative models of open and semi-open-list systems. The risk with lists, of course, is that they can result in tighter party control over who is elected, which runs against the semi-detached relationship to party politics which seems to be desirable in a replacement for the Lords.

There are, however, other debates to be had around an elected Lords:

› Should Lords be elected for long terms, perhaps ten or fifteen years, without the chance of re-election? It would certainly give them more independence from parties and party whips, but it would also reduce their accountability to those who elected them.

› When should elections be held? If on the same day as general elections, turnout would be higher, but so would the likelihood that voters would be influenced by the general election campaigns and a separate decision on the second chamber would risk being swamped, as local elections taking place on general election days are. Would elections at the same time as those for the European Parliament be a better option? Timing them at general elections is most likely to produce a situation where the government is the largest party but without an overall majority, probably the situation where a revising second chamber works best.

› How do we (and should we) retain space for crossbenchers who play a valuable role in the Lords at present? Few of them would be able to mount strong enough election campaigns to win seats as independents (although any voting system should make the election of independents possible). One option would be to allow a sort of 'None of the Above' line on the ballot, and the proportion voting for this would determine or affect the proportion of appointed members in the second chambers.

› Advocates of an un-elected Lords point to the calibre and experience of many members in the present chamber. Would elections lead to a loss in expertise? Here we would argue that expertise should always be available to both chambers, but that is different from deciding who our representatives with the power to vote are. Even an elected chamber could summon the expertise it needs for particular debates, and people like Lords Avebury, Judd and Hylton, to name but a few, who do excellent work in raising issues in a non-party way might be invited to continue as non-voting members.

There is one area of debate, however, which is an important one for electoral reformers. Opponents of Lords reform argue that an elected upper chamber would have, or at least claim to have, greater legitimacy and it would therefore be more inclined to challenge the supremacy of the Commons. There is, however, a degree of ingenuousness about this argument: it is often those who advance it who, when the Lords do their job and obstruct decisions of the Commons, protest that the Lords are merely an unelected appendage. They can't have it both ways – they can't object to the Lords taking decisions because it is unelected but at the same time object to it being elected. They are happy to have a second chamber as long as it is toothless; it is disguised unicameralism.

However, they are not entirely wrong. An elected second chamber might be more assertive, although that is not necessarily a bad thing – many countries have second chambers which have powers that are near equal, but complementary, to those of the lower chamber. If, however, the Commons were to perceive the Lords as being more representative, would it not increase the pressure on the Commons to make itself a more representative body?

Achieving a second chamber elected, or largely elected, by a proportional system is therefore a goal worth striving for in its own right and it would be yet another tier of government not elected by FPTP. It could also, however, help push the Commons towards its own reform. The campaign for Lords reform therefore merits reformers' support.

The government's gradual House of Lords reforms as proposed in 2011 offer a feasible mechanism for democratising the House of Lords and it is probably over this measure that Labour reformers should swallow their distaste for this government and dislike of half-measures, and help those within the government who are serious about reform. After all, the government's plans are not so very different from those which emerged from inquiries and governmental policy proposals during Labour's term of office. Matters such as long non-renewable terms and the precise electoral system (provided it is proportional) should not be pretexts for scuppering the process. The result would be to allow winner-takes-all control to continue indefinitely at Westminster.

Local government has possibilities for the future of electoral reform. It is potentially fairly easy for several reasons:

› Local government in two out of the four nations of the UK (Northern Ireland and Scotland) is already elected by STV, so arguments about its unfamiliarity and unworkability can be easily dismissed. Research on local government in Scotland has shown that STV works well.
› Local government in England and Wales, furthermore, is accustomed to situations in which no party has an overall majority on the council. The 2008 elections in Wales produced four out of twenty-two councils with an overall majority. Most local authorities in England have had a fairly recent period of no overall control and some have had continuous 'hung council' status for very long periods – Sefton in Merseyside continuously since 1986.
› Single-member wards are the exception, not the rule, in local government in England and Wales. The predominant pattern is the three-member ward, although there are many local variations. Three-member wards are found in both the main patterns of election for councils: 'by thirds' (i.e. one third of the members coming

up for each of three years in a four-year cycle, like the metropolitan boroughs) and 'all-out' (like the London boroughs). Arguments about the supposed strength of the single-member representative link therefore do not apply. Three-member STV elections would be a lot less complicated to introduce in most of England than they were in Scotland, which had previously had single-member wards.

› Councils do not produce 'strong government' on the same model as that frequently claimed for Westminster. In most cases their mode of operation is more consensual. The idea of 'strong government' is particularly absurd in cases where there is a separate directly elected mayor, in which case the council is not responsible for the executive at all. Its functions of scrutiny are, indeed, probably better conducted where there is not a majority for the mayor's party on the council. The directly elected mayoral model is increasingly favoured – even imposed – by central government on England and a proportionally elected council seems essential if there is to be any check on or scrutiny of mayoral power.

› Local government is frequently subjected to reform and experiment in its governance and electoral arrangements, as the history of structural reform, Cabinet government and elected mayors demonstrates. Central governments feel free to impose their blueprints on local authorities, usually in the guise of some sort of rhetorical 'localism'. There is thus absolutely no barrier in convention or practice to changing council electoral systems as a government sees fit.

› Having noted central government's ability and willingness to meddle in local government, if a government were to be really serious about devolving power to localities it would be best if there were representative and accountable structures there to receive power – rather than small local elites.

› The councillor's role is based, more than that of the MP, on casework. Electors may want to approach a councillor for whom they voted, or choose between a councillor of the opposition or the administration parties. This choice is available haphazardly at present, in the more marginal seats (either because they are close enough to have split representation in all-out elections, or produce different winning parties at different stages of the electoral cycle). It could usefully be extended.

› The case for reform of the local government electoral system has been upheld in inquiries and reports, particularly the Sunderland Commission in Wales. It was an option that won some support from the Councillors' Commission in England in 2009.

As well as these principled reasons, there are also some pragmatic reasons why local government electoral reform is a feasible next step forward.

› It does not, unlike Westminster (Lords or Commons) choose or help choose its own electoral system. Reforming it does not therefore involve persuading the proverbial turkeys to vote for Christmas. All it requires is for Westminster to legislate in the case of England or the Welsh Assembly to legislate for Wales.

› Local elections follow the national trends in party popularity, so that it is usual for the opposition party to control most of local government by the time a general election produces a change of national government. The Conservatives controlled most of English local government after the 2009 elections, just as Labour ran a large number of councils in 1996. Looking further back, incoming governments in 1970, 1974 and 1979 have all experienced the same pattern. The pendulum then swings in the other direction, with the new opposition party making gains in successive sets of local elections. The early years of a government are therefore not propitious for reforming the electoral system, but the case becomes progressively easier as the government remains in office. By 2009 there were few vested Labour interests in majoritarian voting systems in local government. The same process is likely to make PR in English local government progressively less objectionable to the Conservatives in any future coalition bargaining.

› In Wales, the Assembly is elected by MMP. While Labour did sufficiently well in 2011 to form a single-party government, the position is not necessarily stable for the full term to 2016 and it is likely that future elections will produce coalition situations, as the Assembly terms starting in 1999 and 2007 both did. Reforming the local government electoral system is a policy that is favoured by the Liberal Democrats and Plaid Cymru, and the Conservatives have shown themselves open to the idea. As in Scotland in 2003–04, it is a concession that Labour at Assembly level can make to a coalition partner.

› The local election calendar is a complicated mess of different sorts of election. Tidy-minded civil servants at the Cabinet Office and the Department of Communities and Local Government have had their eye on simplifying it for some time. It would be simple, given a little political will, to put the electoral system into the mix as well.

The Councillors' Commission (under Jane Roberts) was one of several bodies (including the Welsh Conservatives in 2007) or commentators to suggest a 'local option' on electoral systems for councils – areas could decide themselves how they should elect councils, by referendum or by vote of the council.

This is not a particularly attractive idea. Local referendums would be costly and unlikely to produce a lively local debate, while leaving the decision to councils is likely to produce change where it is least needed (in councils that are already under no overall control) and not where it is most needed (where there is a large majority for one party).

FPTP in Welsh local government will probably be the next domino to fall after the second chamber (provided that gets through) – it seems unlikely to survive more than two more Assembly terms. Next would be PR in English local authorities with elected mayors, where the case is particularly obvious and the proposition has the air of a feasible coalition compromise no matter which main party leads the government. The rest of English local government would be an obvious thing for a government in its middle to late period in office to legislate for, or offer to a coalition partner, in order to break up the opposition's municipal strongholds.

Conclusion
The route map to further reform for the House of Commons is constrained but not impossible. Unless other dramatic events supervene, a 'modest proposal' type of reform seems most likely to emerge as a referendum proposition. In the

next chapter we consider what form that modest proposal might take. But the reforming momentum is far from dead in terms of replacing the House of Lords, and possibilities will emerge for local government in England and Wales and any English regional or national bodies that might be created.

Chapter 8

A Winnable Reform

AV has been so resoundingly defeated that it is inconceivable that we will see another referendum on AV, at least for a long time to come. So if we have another referendum, what alternative will be offered to FPTP?

There is a multiplicity of possible electoral systems, but the decision can be narrowed down by asking a few questions of what one wants the system to do and what properties of a proposed system will give it the maximum chance of being implemented. To recapitulate, it needs to survive:

› The legislative process at Westminster
› A referendum campaign.

No matter how good a system may be in principle, it is useless to propose it in Britain (unless there are extraordinary developments like the writing of a full new constitution) unless it can navigate both these constraints. As we have seen in the previous chapter, both constraints reduce the options hugely. In this chapter, we ask some questions of principle and then consider the constraints, before coming to a conclusion as to what sort of system would be the best achievable.

› Do we want a system that is proportional or one that is not?
› If a proportional system, what type?
› And if a proportional system, what degree of proportionality do we want?

Once we have taken these decisions, the choice of system is much narrower and easier.

1. Proportionality or not?

A proportional system is one that, at least to some extent, ensures that a party's share of the seats is related to its share of the votes. While a non-proportional system may by chance produce a reasonably proportional outcome, it cannot be guaranteed to do so. A system that cannot provide an element of proportionality will not overcome some of the more serious defects of FPTP and a third of those who voted Yes in the referendum gave as a main reason for doing so the hope that AV would eventually lead to change to something proportional (and 5 per cent of No voters were hoping for a change to PR in the future as well). The same polling found that 14 per cent of No voters and 49 per cent of Yes voters would have supported PR in a referendum that gave the option.

That would appear to point us to a proportional system. However, many who voted Yes did so believing that AV would be fairer than FPTP while remaining opposed to proportional representation. Non-proportional systems cannot therefore be ruled out of our thinking without a little further consideration.

If we decide we don't want even a modestly proportional system, however, we face a difficulty in that there are few realistic options. Indeed, other than FPTP and AV, there is only one non-proportional system that merits consideration: the Supplementary Vote (SV). As the system we use for mayoral elections, it has the merit of being a system already in use and perhaps might prove more immune to some of the attacks from which AV suffered

The SV differs from AV in two respects: while with AV voters can, if they so wish, rank all candidates in their preferred order, SV voters can only express a first and second choice, and if no candidate has over 50 per cent of first-choice votes, then all candidates other than the leading two are eliminated.

Other than in three-way marginals SV will nearly always produce the same results as AV, but the more limited choice can present a dilemma for some voters. A Green voter, for example, may want to give their first preference to a Green candidate even if that candidate has little hope of winning. But suppose the constituency is a three-way marginal with the Conservatives, Labour and the Liberal Democrats all in contention. The Green voter may give a second preference for, say, the Liberal Democrat only to find that the second round is only between Labour and the Conservatives – the vote is therefore wasted. This is not a theoretical problem – surprisingly many mayoral elections have had only a narrow gap between the second and fourth placed candidates on the first count.

However, not having all the benefits of AV, SV would be even more of a compromise for those seeking meaningful reform, and we doubt that it would be enough of a reform to generate the enthusiasm that winning a referendum would require. It is a pity that the AV referendum seems to have closed off the possibility of just legislating for a very small reform like SV. Because SV is such a small change, it may be just about possible to introduce it on a 'sale or return' basis, as with Europe in 1973–75, with a trial period of the reform before the referendum.

2. What sort of proportional system?

If we want a proportional system there are only two broad types that need concern us – they are:

> Systems that use multi-member constituencies (sometimes referred to as electoral regions or districts);
> Hybrid systems that elect MPs in single-member constituencies and then award additional seats to parties that suffer from the disproportionality of single-member constituency outcomes. In the academic literature these are referred to as Mixed Member Proportional, or MMP, but the MMP systems we use in Britain for devolved government are often (unsatisfactorily) known as AMS.

To guarantee some level of proportionality, more than one candidate must be elected in the area in which the election is held. With only constituencies in which a single member is elected, a party that narrowly wins in every constituency (to take an extreme case) could win all the seats in spite of having nowhere near a majority of the votes – that is why FPTP, AV and SV are not proportional. Systems that elect several members at a time can be designed so that the plurality winner does not take all and that other points of view are represented.

There are two ways in which we can elect more than one candidate at the same time: we can use multi-member constituencies or MMP systems that elect members in single-member constituencies and then award 'additional' members to compensate parties that suffer from the disproportionality of these single-member elections.

Multi-member constituency systems
There are two basic sorts of multi-member system, depending on whether parties or candidates are the basic unit of competition.

Party List PR is a very flexible sort of system: indeed, it may be a mistake to see it as a 'system' at all because there are so many variations on the same basic idea of parties putting forward lists of their candidates. One can have some quite small local districts (as in Spain), regional (as in Britain's elections for MEPs) or national lists (as in Israel). Some electoral systems, such as Denmark's, have local and national 'tiers' of representation. They also vary as to how the order of candidates elected is determined – if a party wins, say, three seats, which three candidates are elected? There are many possibilities.

We already use a list system for electing MEPs (other than in Northern Ireland). In each region, parties stand lists of candidates. The votes a party receives determines how many seats a party wins. If a party wins three seats, then the three top candidates on that party's list are elected. This sort of list is called a 'closed' list because the choice of candidates is closed to the voter. For that reason, closed lists would be unsatisfactory for general elections in Britain, because people expect and are used to voting for a particular individual to represent them. Closed lists would give too much power to the party's own structures in determining who sits in parliament – rebels could be consigned to the bottom of the list if they fall out with the whips, and therefore fail to be re-elected even if they are popular with the voters.

There is more merit to other possible ways of organising lists: 'open' (in which the order of candidates elected is entirely determined by the preferences expressed by voters) or 'semi-open' (in which the party chooses an order but it can be altered by the voters). Voters in countries such as Finland (completely open), Denmark (semi-open) and Spain (closed but local) all seem happy with their list systems. But list PR is too radical a change from Britain's particular experience, which values constituency representation and individual accountability, and its chances of winning a referendum would be very low.

The Single Transferable Vote is the other sort of multi-member constituency system. With STV parties can stand several candidates in each multi-member constituency, but voters vote by ranking the candidates, just as they would do in an AV election (AV is the single-seat variant of STV). But whereas with AV a candidate must pass 50 per cent of the votes to be elected, with STV they must reach a 'quota' which is the total number of votes divided by one more than the number of candidates to be elected. In electing four candidates, for example, the quota is 20 per cent (a fifth), because if four candidates each get at least 20 per cent of the votes then no other candidate can get more than 20 per cent.

With AV, if no candidate has more than 50 per cent of the votes, the candidate with the fewest votes is eliminated and their votes are transferred to the next candidates on the ballot papers. With STV, however, 'surplus' votes are first transferred from candidates who have more than a quota. STV counts *are* complicated to administer. Although it is done manually in Ireland, it takes some time; in Scottish local elections it is counted electronically. However, from the voter's point of view STV is pretty simple – you vote '1' for your first choice candidate, '2' for second choice and so on until you are indifferent between the remaining options – just like AV. But STV will often involve getting a choice between different candidates of the same party.

STV is more familiar than list PR in Anglophone countries; it has been used for all elections in the Republic of Ireland since independence, and it is used in Malta and for some elections in Australia – and one or two in the United States. It is used in the UK for all Northern Ireland elections, except for MPs, and for local authorities in Scotland. It has been recommended by official inquiries for use in Welsh local government and the Welsh Assembly, and highlighted for future consideration for the Scottish Parliament and English local government. It was used for electing university MPs in 1918–50. It has been the principal goal of the British electoral reform movement since the establishment of the Electoral Reform Society (then the 'Proportional Representation Society') in 1884.

Like list PR, STV's properties can vary. The main consideration is the size of constituencies. Small constituencies offer local representation, but are less proportional overall; large constituencies can dilute local representation but offer voters more choice of candidate. STV in the Australian Senate has an adaptation involving casting a party vote, which converts it into something like a list system; STV in Malta has a sort of 'additional member' top-up.

Mixed systems aka Additional Member System

These systems are a hybrid of two electoral systems: FPTP is used to elect members in single-member constituencies (as at present), and a list mechanism is used to elect 'regional' or 'additional' members. The principal type of mixed system, **Mixed Member Proportional (MMP)**, uses a list election to compensate for the disproportionality of FPTP. With most forms of MMP, parties stand single candidates in the constituencies and a list of candidates in each region. Voters get two votes – one to elect the constituency MP and the second for the party they want to win. Once the constituency votes have been counted, the additional seats are awarded to parties to achieve a result as near as possible to a proportional outcome based on the party votes.

In Britain, MMP is used for the Scottish Parliament and the Welsh and London Assemblies; it is the established system in Germany and was the outcome of the well-considered reform process in New Zealand in the early 1990s.

AV+ is another of the possible variants of the MMP principle. Recommended by the Jenkins Commission, it uses AV rather than FPTP in the constituency contests. To give voters some say in which list members will be elected, it also recommended that semi-open lists rather than closed be used. However, while the Commission made a valiant effort to come up with a solution that would be politically acceptable, AV+, involving one vote in which voters rank candidates and another in which they vote with a cross for either a party or a candidate on a party's list, is open to attack on the grounds of its complexity for voters.

A commission set up by the Hansard Society in 1976 recommended a form of MMP that requires only one vote. They proposed that rather than voters giving a second 'party' or 'regional' vote, the votes in the constituencies should be used to determine the overall proportionality that the system should aim for, hence the allocation of additional seats. However, it ignores the problem of, say, Green voters who may not have a constituency candidate or who may want to vote tactically in the constituency contest but thereby deny their party the chance of a list seat.

Not MMP, but still within the broad-brush definition of AMS, is the **'Mixed Member Majoritarian'** (**MMM**) or parallel electoral system used in Japan and Korea, and (effectively) in Italy between 1994 and 2005. The list seats are allocated without reference to the constituency seats each party has won. This has some interesting properties; it will produce much more majoritarian results than MMP, but still modify a FPTP result to give a voice in Parliament to parties that are under-represented or excluded.

Another system that belongs in the MMP family is **Total Representation (TR)**. This is a new system, proposed by Aharon Nathan, and one that has yet to be used, but that should not prevent us from considering it. As a new system, it deserves a more extended introduction as the properties of other systems ('regular' MMP, STV, AV and so on) are well covered elsewhere. Some further analysis of TR is given in the Appendix.

From the voter's end of the process, TR is exactly the same as FPTP. The familiar ballot paper listing local candidates, marking an X by the candidate to whom one is entrusting one's vote: these would all be identical. Just as in FPTP, the candidate with a plurality of votes (even if far short of a majority) is elected MP for the constituency.

The difference comes with what happens to the votes cast for losing candidates, which in recent UK general elections accounts for a majority of votes cast. These are then pooled and used to elect top-up MPs; TR is therefore a member of the MMP 'family' although with a single vote that 'transfers' from candidate to party if the candidate is not elected.

As with other MMP systems, the numbers of MPs elected from constituency and party votes can be adjusted for greater or lesser proportionality, although it is probably not as suitable as regular two-ballot MMP for producing results at the proportional end of the spectrum (40 per cent plus from lists as in Scotland and Germany).

The pool of otherwise 'wasted' votes used for electing the top-up MPs can be based on local, regional or national levels. The original version (based on experience in Israel) involved a single national pool, but in UK circumstances the largest feasible groupings are probably the four nations, and public acceptance might be greater if there were an element of regional or local pooling. Seats would be allocated proportionally, based on the votes received by that party's initially unsuccessful candidates, and the individuals elected on each party ticket would be that party's candidates with the largest number (or maybe percentage) of votes.

The idea of using pooled 'wasted' votes rather than a separate list vote has an elegant simplicity about it. It would, hopefully, accord with an intuitive sense of fairness; the referendum campaign failed to persuade people that preferential voting was fairer and better. While TR as such is a new system, pooling unused votes is a feature of several European electoral systems such as the Danish one (although in that case fairly small list-PR districts, rather than single-seat FPTP districts, are the lowest tier of representation).

The simplicity comes, as one might imagine, at a price. It is not as friendly as regular MMP to the smaller parties (although this depends a bit on the details of implementation). The true level of support might be suppressed: for example, UKIP supporters may still choose to vote tactically (probably for the Conservatives) because the constituency seats are the dominant way in which MPs are elected. Particularly if localised top-up districts (like counties) were involved, the threshold for electing top-up MPs is fairly high for small parties, although TR does produce strikingly fairer results between the principal four (or three in England) parties. It does not eliminate the penalty that a tendency in public opinion pays for being split between competing parties. It also does not do anything about 'surpluses' – large majorities for candidates in safe seats, and the lack of incentive for supporters of the locally dominant party to turn out (supporters of the weaker parties, incidentally, *do* have such an incentive because it helps elect top-up MPs).

TR is not dissimilar in effect to the AV+ system recommended by the Jenkins report in 1998, but streamlined (FPTP rather than AV for the constituency seats, and no complicated open-list ballot for the top-up seats).

Choosing between multi-member constituency and mixed systems
Both multi-member constituency and mixed systems have much to recommend them, and for that reason we do not discount either, but both would present different sets of problems and opportunities when it comes to campaigning.

Most politicians dislike multi-member-constituency systems because they 'break the link' between MPs and their constituents. At present each constituency elects a unique MP whose job it is to represent all their constituents. If more than one MP represents a wider constituency, then that uniqueness is lost and more than one MP may speak, perhaps with different voices, on behalf of constituents. The argument, however, is generally made by MPs and those close to them who enjoy a monopolistic position in their constituencies with no rivals to express opinions different to their own. In every other field of endeavour MPs tell us that competition is good, but when it comes to democracy they decide it does not apply to them.

If more than one MP represents an area then electors have more choice. Someone requiring the services of an MP may then decide to raise their problems with an MP of the party of their choice – a Labour supporter will feel more comfortable talking to a Labour MP, a Conservative with a Conservative, etc. Some may prefer to discuss their problems with a woman MP, others with a man, or perhaps with someone of their own ethnic background if such an MP is available.

Moreover, while MPs can represent all of their constituents at present in the sense that they can attend to the casework generated by constituents, whatever their political views, there is no way that a single MP can represent all constituents politically. An MP has just one vote in the Commons, but how they vote will not reflect the views of many of their constituents. With more than one MP, there is more chance that all significant views in a constituency will be represented in Parliament. Thus while single-member constituencies might be good for MPs, multi-member constituencies have many more advantages for voters (although opinion polls show that voters, at least at present, still prefer the simplicity of single-member constituencies and however illogical that might appear it is something to be reckoned with when planning a campaign).

Another argument made against multi-member constituencies is that they make it more difficult for MPs to know well the wider areas they must represent. If the total number of MPs were to remain the same, a three-member constituency, for example, would be three times as large as a present constituency. This argument has more validity, but these days when most constituency casework is conducted by telephone or email, the problems in dealing with larger constituencies can be overstated.

Supporters of mixed systems claim that they are preferable because they retain single-member constituencies, but this is only partly true. Take the Scottish Parliament as an example: each constituency is represented by eight members – a single constituency member, but also seven members from lists who also represent the wider region. Moreover, while the voting system creates a direct accountability of the constituency member to the electors in the constituency, the regional members, who owe their positions to where the parties placed them on their lists, are only weakly linked to the people they represent.

Another problem with mixed systems is that they create two categories of member – constituency and regional members. Both have equal status in parliament, but the electorate perceives them very differently. Surveys in Scotland show that most electors have little knowledge of who their regional members are or what they are supposed to do. They are regarded as 'second-class' members, in many cases elected although they lost in constituencies where they were also candidates (not in Wales, however, where candidates can stand for a constituency or on a list, but not both – this solves one problem but creates more for smaller parties which may rely on lists for representation but find that their leaders cannot risk contesting constituencies).

Changing to an MMP system would, however, present a practical difficulty. If present (or revised) constituency boundaries were to be retained, adding regional members would significantly increase the number of MPs and there is no public appetite for that. To introduce a highly proportional MMP system without an overall increase in the number of MPs would require a fairly severe cut in the number of constituencies. However, we advocate a relatively small ratio of regional to constituency seats as we believe only a modest degree of proportionality is achievable, but a small ratio would also have the advantage of minimising the boundary changes that would be needed. The government is already reducing the number of constituencies to 600 and proposes a boundary review in every future parliament, so MPs have already imposed instability in boundaries. A one-off further cut in constituencies to 550 and 100 top-up seats (bringing Parliament back to the size it is in 2010–15) would produce 15.4 per cent of MPs chosen from the top-up mechanism, a modest amount similar to the Jenkins proposal.

3. How proportional should – or can – the electoral system be?

At one end of the scale we can go for 'pure proportionality' in which the percentage of seats a party wins is as close as it possibly can be to the percentage of the votes it receives, but at the other we can go for a small degree of proportionality giving only a measure of protection against highly disproportional outcomes.

All the 'PR' systems (lists, STV and mixed) can be more, or less, proportional depending on their precise design.

› In general, the more members elected at the same time, the more proportional the system. STV based on 6-member seats as in Northern Ireland is more proportional than the 3–4 member version in Scottish local government. MMP with 40 per cent or more elected from lists gives pretty accurate proportionality, while with 33 per cent (as in Wales) it is more majoritarian and with 15–20 per cent as with AV+ and TR it is a representative tweak to a basically majoritarian system. National list PR is more proportional than regional list PR.

› Electoral systems can impose specific thresholds by which parties need to obtain a minimum percentage of the vote (or number of constituency seats) to qualify for proportionality. In the Netherlands this threshold is 0.67 per cent; in Israel 2 per cent; in Germany and London it is 5 per cent; in Turkey it is 10 per cent, with a requirement that a party gain significant votes in more than one province.

› PR systems can be engineered to give an explicit winner's bonus for the largest party or electoral alliance, as the systems in Greece and Italy do. Arguments often used to justify FPTP are often stronger if deployed in favour of such 'reinforced PR' options.

› Some more abstruse system details can also alter proportionality at the edges – the ability of parties to form electoral alliances or the averaging method used to award seats.[67]

›

In producing a legislative body like the House of Commons there are several valid considerations which may conflict with each other. Proportionality as such is usually considered to be a desirable quality – nobody would argue for a system in which votes cast and seats won were completely unrelated to each other – but advocates of majoritarian systems like FPTP and AV believe that other considerations put limits on

---

67   D'Hondt involves a higher threshold than the other commonly used formulae, and largest remainders a lower threshold.

the degree of proportionality that is desirable. For an FPTP supporter, other considerations outweigh proportionality to such a degree that quite extreme disproportionality is tolerable (or even desirable).

The debate over proportionality is usually quite unnecessarily polarised. Nobody would argue for a system in which votes cast and seats won were completely unrelated to each other, and likewise among electoral reformers is no appetite for taking proportionality to its absolute conclusion of, for instance, having UK-wide list PR and giving a party with 1/650 of the votes (0.15 per cent) a seat in the House of Commons. To have PR or not to have PR is not the question – the question is one of degree. Even the term 'proportional representation' has become unhelpful, artificially dividing the political community into supporters and opponents of PR.

So, whatever system we choose, we can also choose a model that does more or less what we want in terms of proportionality. The issue is how to make a choice that provides a reform worth working for and at the same time does not generate a level of opposition that makes a referendum impossible to win.

› **What is the threshold for winning a majority of seats?** Under FPTP, as we saw in 2005, 35 per cent can be enough and this is surely low enough to cause concern. But most PR systems do not mechanically require 50 per cent, and allow majorities if a party has more than 40 per cent and a clear lead over its nearest rival. For instance, the SNP won a majority in the Scottish Parliament MMP election in 2011 with 44 per cent, and Labour had a majority in Glasgow in 2007 with 43 per cent of the vote under STV. This is reasonable, particularly if the opposing parties do not represent a coherent ideological point of view or potential government.

> **What sort of consent is required to govern?** This is a somewhat complicated question, as consent comes in several forms. One is a kind of generalised consent to the system and the results it produces. The classic two-party FPTP system could be said to enjoy this sort of consent – that two parties with 44–49 per cent would periodically exchange office, recognise each other's authority to govern for that parliamentary term and over the long term enjoy a sort of 'proportionality of power'. Another sort of consent is given through AV – although a party is well short of majority support on first preferences, it can demonstrate a broader type of approval through lower preferences. Another is from coalition government, in which two or more parties, without majorities, agree a compromise joint programme (although the coalition agreement may not end up reflecting majority preferences).

> **What should be the threshold for gaining representation?** There is hardly a proposition, no matter how offensive or ridiculous, that is not capable of gaining 1 or 2 per cent in an opinion poll. Translating such fragments into seats may involve breaking up representation too far, making it difficult to gather a majority in Parliament and also perhaps lowering the dignity and effectiveness of a nation's Parliament. By failing to deter fragmentation, representation of tiny parties also undermines the vital role of larger parties in aggregating interests and deciding priorities. However, there is also the desirability of representing serious political positions with significant numbers of adherents in the national debate, as without

them Parliament is not representative; putting the barriers to entry to the political market-place too high can also lead to staleness and elitism. Some PR systems (like Germany's) impose a formal threshold; some have an effective threshold because they only elect a few people at a time from small districts (like Scottish STV or Spanish lists).

> **What sort of local representation should there be?** A single national list may be the most proportional option but it is rare because in most political systems there is a need for local representation and accountability. Completely national lists probably result in an unacceptable disconnection between politicians and electors. Local representation exposes politicians more to 'real life'; and they also enable clear representation of the different needs of different parts of the polity. With national lists, localised concerns (a riot, a factory closure etc.) are everyone's problem and therefore nobody's problem. Single member systems involve the most local form of representation, but on the other hand a monopoly of local representation on the basis, usually, of a minority of local support. Multi-member seats, and mixed systems, involve some loss of locality but an increase in representativeness and choice. If more than one MP represents an area then electors have more choice – both in terms of the voting decision and whom to approach between elections.

There is no shortage of academic literature on the finer points of system design but, as we saw with the AV referendum, in practice the choices are more likely to emerge from the gut instincts and self-interest of politicians.

4. What are the viable options?

British political culture puts a high priority on local representation and votes for individuals rather than parties. Bearing this in mind, and the 'referendum' and 'Westminster' constraints outlined in the previous chapter, a modest change rather than a radical shift to a highly proportional system is most likely to emerge from a future reform process. Such a modest reform would involve a strong element of localised representation, a candidate-centred electoral system, a fairly high threshold to representation and a fairly low threshold for forming a single-party majority government.

We can rapidly conclude that a list-PR system is not the answer. This leaves three broad possibilities:

> A non-proportional system, such as AV or SV.
> Multi-member STV constituencies, based on small constituencies (a norm of three members) to produce the most local degree of representation and a fairly majoritarian national outcome.
> A mixed system relying mainly on single member constituencies with a small amount of top-up representation (15–20 per cent), like TR, AV+, MMM or the usual type of MMP.

>

Another consideration intrudes at this point – simplicity. Britain has a regrettably anti-intellectual culture, particularly about anything with a hint of science or mathematics about it, and this affects what is winnable in a referendum. In the AV referendum the No campaign tried, successfully but dishonestly, to portray AV as a complicated system. The Yes campaign made some avoidable errors in responding, but the No forces were working with the grain of public prejudice and this has to be taken into account.

In reality, the British are of course perfectly capable of using other voting systems, in Scotland, Wales and Northern Ireland doing so routinely. Irish voters have a fairly sophisticated understanding of STV, and Scandinavians take pretty complicated variants of list PR in their stride.[68] It is frustrating that public discourse in the UK is so debased, but it is something which must be taken into account if one wants to win a referendum. Keeping it simple is therefore useful; AV+ falls at this hurdle.

The simplest sort of system consistent with any degree of reform at all is a single-ballot mixed system like TR or Hansard-style MMP. SV might just qualify as well. Depending on the circumstances, going a bit further than this (small-district STV or regular MMP with only 10–20 per cent of list MPs) might be a practical proposition, but a minimalist, simple reform should always be borne in mind as a backstop. These sorts of reform may even manage to keep the same sort of coalition as AV; opponents of full proportionality may be prepared to put up with a majoritarian version of PR, such as TR or even small-district STV, as a compromise with pro-PR reformers.

Conclusion: two options
We would like to put forward two possible propositions for

---

68 My own favoured electoral system, in an ideal world, would be a sort of 'STV+' based on small-district STV (1–4 members, with most having 2–3), as below. There would be a small top-up tier to ensure that parties with significant but thinly spread support had a voice in parliament, and that the relationship between first preferences and votes was made a little closer. Several political scientists thought something like this was the best solution for the electoral reform needs of the Netherlands in the mid-2000s. The complex Danish system also has considerable merit. But the chances of introducing either from a standing start in the UK are nil. (LB)

the future, which would be feasible referendum-winners. If the way forward is via a committee of inquiry, or a 'sale or return' trial reform followed by a referendum, other options might open up again. One does not want to be prescriptive – what is important is that the next referendum is fought on a system that is substantially better than FPTP, that stands a good chance of winning and around which electoral reformers can unite.

1. Small-district STV

STV in small districts would involve multi-member constituencies with perhaps usually 2–3 members and, depending on local geography, the odd exceptions with one or four MPs such as island seats and cities of a certain size (Bristol). These would be multiples of existing constituencies, although a future boundary review could bring them more accurately into line with local authority and community boundaries. While there are practical difficulties involved in, say, organising and representing a six-member seat covering all of Bedfordshire, these are much less if we are talking about two three-member seats, one for Luton and the south west and one for Bedford and the middle and north of the county.

Voting, as under AV, is preferential, offering voters a much more flexible way of expressing their views. When people use preferential voting, they grasp the principle and make effective use of the system's possibilities – as demonstrated in the Scottish local elections under STV in 2007.

Small-district STV will tend to produce fairly proportional results; it is better at evening things up between the major parties than representing new parties. The model result in the Appendix gives a very proportional result for 2010.

However, it would enable a party with a particularly strong tide in its favour to win a parliamentary majority.

However, the usual implementation of STV would mean (as in many Scottish local elections using 3–4 member STV) that the potential benefits for voter choice and social equality will not be felt, because most parties would nominate only one candidate. However, the system can be adapted to compensate for the small size of districts. For example, a rule requiring parties standing more than one candidate to field at least one woman (and at least one man) would see more women on ballot papers. A rule requiring a party that won more than, say, 20 per cent in one election to nominate multiple candidates in the next election would heighten this effect. Moreover, if vacancies were to be filled by recounts of the original votes but ignoring preferences for the candidate who had deceased or resigned (which would also have the advantage of preserving proportionality which can be lost in by-elections), then all parties would have an incentive to stand more than one candidate in case they won a seat only to lose it through their candidate suffering from a heart attack: not only would this lead to more women candidates, but more voters would be able to choose between alternative candidates of their preferred party.

Small-district STV is therefore a feasible compromise, lying at the proportional end of our spectrum of feasibility.

2. Small top-up MMP (TR)

If simplicity is necessary to get a system through a referendum, then the ingenious TR scores well and has advantages over other variants of MMP. It is more majoritarian than small-district STV because most of its seats are decided by FPTP. A party winning a large majority under FPTP would therefore always win under TR, even if it obtained no compensatory seats (and there would usually be sufficient unsuccessful candidates of the victorious party to qualify for some top-up seats).

For the voter, it is identical to FPTP, so no one can argue it is complicated. It cannot be subjected to the same sort of misrepresentation and mystification as preferential voting was in the AV campaign. The idea of voting 1, 2, 3 is simple enough, but the problems came in explaining how the vote was actually used under AV. It was easy enough for the No campaign to give an exaggerated impression of how complicated it would actually be, and there were also more valid questions among the politically interested public. For instance, it is not obvious why second and third preferences count, when transferred, at full value rather than at a lower strength than first preferences. It could also be unfairly portrayed as empowering supporters of the smallest parties more than the mainstream or – the subject of much portentous and ignorant comment – not giving one person one vote. But these arguments could not be easily knocked down in a referendum campaign.

It may do nothing to get rid of safe seats, but even in safe seats votes for losing candidates would still have value as they could help parties win 'additional' seats and, through these 'additional' seats, a measure of proportionality could be achieved – a goal that AV itself would not have delivered.

TR achieves some of the same benefits as small-district STV, in that it reduces the polarisation of representation that FPTP produces. Southern Labour, urban and Scottish Conservatives, and Liberal Democrats in most areas, would gain some representatives of their choice. Depending on whether the compensatory seats are awarded at local, regional or national level, it can be more or less friendly to the smaller parties. National-level TR would set a pretty low threshold for representation (perhaps 2 per cent or less), local-level pretty high (not much less than in AV) (see Appendix for details). Given British political culture and the Westminster and referendum constraints, a form of TR based on counties or regions would stand a better chance of winning.

The argument about AV was often couched in terms of the dilemma of the tactical voter, something which was not relevant to a large number of electors. TR, on the other hand, provides a better answer than AV to Matthew Taylor's persuasive question about electoral systems:

> My view was simple. The strongest argument for AV is that it makes more voters matter. So, the campaign should find three real people each of whom should combine a winning personality with a proper job, say a taxi driver, a shopkeeper and a nurse. The taxi driver would be a Labour voter in Surrey; the nurse would be a Tory in Barnsley and the shop keeper a Liberal Democrat in South Wales. The whole campaign would be about Fred, Ahmed and Rita and why they would continue to be ignored by all the parties as long as first past the post persists. In every debate the 'yes' side would simply demand from the 'no' side what they would say to Fred, Ahmed and Rita who had never been canvassed, never got a leaflet and never voted for a winning general election candidate.[69]

Even against the depressing background of the AV referendum, it is never too soon to begin discussions about what the next attempt to reform the electoral system

---

69 http://www.matthewtaylorsblog.com/thersa/too-clever-for-this-world/

should look like – and, just as important, what a successful referendum campaign would look like.

We know that our recommendation of STV based on three-member constituencies, or an MMP system with at the very most 20 per cent of the seats as regional seats, will not meet the approval of many electoral reformers who have argued long and hard for something much better than that. For them, what we propose may appear timid. However, our inclination is to go for a battle that can be won, and in our judgement that means accepting that many are opposed to greater proportionality, even if we consider their arguments not to be strong ones, and going some way to meeting their concerns.

In electoral reform circles it has often been said that the best should not be the enemy of the good: in the past we have rejected this view as an argument that leads us to advocating a system that does not meet all the criteria we would regard as desirable, but the experience of recent years and the defeat of AV leads us to the view that we should aim not for the best system, but the best we can get. That may well be a simplified, majoritarian sort of MMP.

Chapter 9

The Next Steps

The AV referendum was a dismal defeat for reformers. Winning was always going to be a challenge, but it was made so much worse by the ill-starred birth of the referendum project (as a desperate wheeze by the Labour government and an unsatisfactory compromise by the coalition parties) and the mistakes made by the Yes campaign.

The biggest dangers for electoral reform after May 2011 are despondency and despair, but there is no need for either. As this book has argued, progress is still possible in other areas, and reform of the House of Commons will return to the agenda well before the complacent predictions of its smug opponents. Although it is important not to overstate how much can be achieved by activism, the Yes campaign did bring together creativity and energy and the gains from that will be apparent over the longer term. As Ken Livingstone remarked about the abolition of the Greater London Council in 1986, the defeat was like knocking the head off a dandelion – the seeds would be carried far and wide and sprout in unexpected ways. It did not seem likely then that Livingstone would be running London again within fourteen years. Nor that ideas (then considered wacky) that had developed within the GLC about sex and race equality, gay rights and accountable policing would have become mainstream by then.

There were other gains from the referendum. Electoral reform is a mainstream cause within the Labour Party.

The Labour leadership came out in favour of reform in a way it has never done before during the referendum; the fact that a referendum was held demonstrates that FPTP is no longer regarded as an immutable part of our constitution.

Discontent with the society we live in, and its rancid, boring politics, runs very high but so do despair and apathy. This book has suggested a number of possible avenues for progress towards a fairer electoral system. There also needs to be a root-and-branch re-examination of how 'progressive' politics works and how the argument for reform can be made. Another opportunity to change from FPTP will surely come, and in this final chapter we consider what now must be done to prepare the ground for the challenge ahead.

Labour

Labour is likely to hold the key to success. With Labour divided on AV in the referendum campaign there was little hope of victory, and in any future referendum the position of the Labour Party and its supporters will be critical.

The arithmetic is clear. With the Conservatives being near to unanimous in their opposition to reform and the much smaller Liberal Democrats in favour, the Yes side can only win if Labour supporters are overwhelmingly for reform. Of course in a referendum voters do not blindly follow the line of their preferred party, but for a great many people what is being said by the political leaders they trust is important. AV would not necessarily have won in 2011 if Labour had united behind it, but without a large majority of Labour supporters AV did not stand a chance. Getting Labour backing for change is therefore vital (unless, of course, the Conservatives see the light and embrace reform, but at present that appears unlikely).

In 2010, however, getting Labour backing was never going to be easy when the Yes campaign was perceived as a Liberal Democrat project. At a time when the Liberal Democrats were in deep political trouble and relations between the Labour and Lib Dem parties were so bad, siding with the Liberal Democrats in the referendum campaign was a step many Labour supporters were not prepared to take. Many preferred to use their vote to 'kick' Nick Clegg, even if that meant voting the same way as David Cameron.

However, even in more favourable political circumstances, getting Labour to back what is seen as a Liberal Democrat campaign will be difficult. The referendum initiative must therefore be Labour's at least as much as it belongs to the Liberal Democrats. That will not be easy, but it is far from impossible.

That Ed Miliband and most of his shadow campaign spoke in favour of AV is hugely encouraging – since the 1929–31 parliament never has there been such a strong public commitment to change. Even in 1931 that stance seemed born of pragmatism and accommodating the Liberals, but in 2011 Ed Miliband's position was part of a sincere commitment to changing the way politics is done. Moreover, those Labour figures who opposed AV were mostly from a previous political generation whose outlook was forged in the 1970s and 1980s, and their influence will wane. Many of those in Labour who wanted AV were still opposed to a proportional system, but that can change. In accepting that FPTP must go, they crossed a rubicon and at least some of them will be ready to engage in a new debate on what should take its place. It is important that the discussion within Labour should acknowledge the existence of the middle position which is in favour of reform but not full PR, and that a measure of proportionality need not be anathema to people with a sincere belief in majoritarian government.

But how is that debate to be won in Labour? The history of electoral reform tells us that progress is only likely to be made through a mix of principle and pragmatism. During the referendum campaign Ed Miliband and his colleagues advanced an argument of principle – they supported AV on the grounds that it would make elections fairer and politics better. We want politics to be based on principle and should not therefore be cynical about politicians who take principled positions – but principles can be electoral assets. When many electors are fed up with politics based on party point-scoring and confrontation, they can be attractive. When in 2009 Labour was considering its position on electoral reform in advance of the 2010 election, opinion polls showed that supporting reform would help Labour among some floating voters who might otherwise have supported the Lib Dems. Electoral reform is never likely to be the prime determinant of how people vote, but taking a stand for a better democracy may just win the few extra seats needed for victory in a tight election contest, for example by attracting Liberal Democrat waverers in Conservative–Labour marginals. Talking about reform can therefore be to Labour's electoral advantage.

Thus for die-hard Labour supporters, there are pragmatic reasons for backing reform. However, there is also a pragmatic argument that might be even more compelling. Establishing Labour as something different from the Labour of 2009/10 is not going to be easy; recovery from an election defeat is usually slow and even in mid-2011 Labour had not yet established more than a slim opinion poll lead. Past loss of office has been followed by further loss of votes (in 1951–55, 1970–74 and 1979–83) – while this need not be repeated, the difficulty of regaining support should not be underestimated. Governments are, with rare exceptions, not turfed out after a single term these days – there is often a sense that a 'fair go' involves a second term for a party – and the coalition parties' strategy of blaming Labour for everything exacerbates the problem.

Labour will find the next election, probably in 2015, a difficult one to win, at least in the sense of winning an outright majority of seats. The politics and the general pattern of electoral history are the most important causes, but the task is made a little harder still with the boundary changes and the reduction in the number of seats which the Liberal Democrats traded for the AV referendum. Unless Labour can open up a very clear lead over the Conservatives, even a weakened Liberal Democrat Party may hold the balance of power in the event of another hung parliament. Labour might have little sympathy for the Liberal Democrats, believing that they are receiving the punishment they deserve for an unprincipled alliance with an old enemy, but the last thing Labour wants is another Conservative-led government come the next election. Labour may still need to look for Liberal Democrat support to prevent that from happening, and support is not likely to be available unless Labour is seen to be at least open to electoral reform.

Partnership with the Liberal Democrats is not, of course, something most Labour supporters will find an attractive proposition, particularly at present. They see the Liberal

Democrats as the people who put the Conservatives into power, allowing them to do so much damage to public services. Many Labour supporters are infuriated by the Liberal Democrats' about-turn on economic policy and their inflated condemnation of Brown's government.

Nevertheless, taking a longer-term view, progressive Liberals share many of Labour's values – on fairness, support for the vulnerable, tax, civil liberties and so on. Labour is still not the sole home for progressive England, still less the only progressive political party of Scotland and Wales. Some progressive Liberal Democrats are hanging on in their current party, trying to make the best of the situation and sometimes ameliorating right-wing policies desired by the Conservatives or indeed their own leadership. Given the difficulties of gaining an overall majority, it would be foolish not to prepare the ground for co-operation with the Lib Dems – hopefully under new leadership and with a refreshed political programme by the time of the next election.

Coalition, or at least some form of pact, with the Liberal Democrats may not be particularly palatable for Labour, but it may be the only way of implementing Labour policies. Labour's experience of coalition with the Liberal Democrats in Scotland from 1999 to 2007 was generally positive: during that period the Scottish Parliament abolished university tuition fees, agreed to pay for the long-term care of the elderly, abolished Clause 28 faster than the rest of the UK, introduced a more extensive right to roam, and brought in freedom of information that went further than the Westminster government would allow. Labour in coalition in Scotland did much more of what many Labour supporters wanted than Tony Blair was able to do (or was prepared to do) with a large Commons majority. Thus while winning the next election outright must remain Labour's aim, should that not be possible, governing in tandem with the Liberal Democrats would not be too bad an alternative, and certainly much better than another term of Conservative government.

Labour needs also to remember that there is a large section of left opinion that is not attached either to it or the Liberal Democrats, and co-operative working is not impossible. Labour's coalition with Plaid Cymru in Wales produced a progressive government, and the relationship between Labour and Green in London politics has also been of immense value. It is depressing that even Peter Hain, a long term advocate of AV, has used the referendum and boundary changes as a pretext for suggesting the use of FPTP for the Welsh Assembly. Such moves need to be fiercely resisted within the Labour Party – it is simply not intelligent to revert to the machine style of politics, aimed at a monopoly of power, that has been one of the least attractive aspects of Labour culture.

However, whether we believe Labour should back electoral reform for reasons of principle or pragmatism, we need to start work now on making the case within the party. Here we suggest a number of approaches.

At national level

Arguing directly for reform of the voting system so soon after the electorate, for whatever reasons, has voted against change is unlikely to get us far. But we can lay the groundwork.

The Labour leader's call for a better form of politics, based on more reasoned debate and in which politicians of different parties do not feel they need to be engaged in endless confrontation, creates possibilities. We must of course expect the government to strongly defend its policies and the opposition to be vigorous in holding them to account but, as Ed Miliband has argued, politicians need to recognise that no one party has a monopoly of good ideas. Voters are fed up with what they see as the constant bickering of politicians engaged in juvenile point-scoring debates and want to see MPs having more reasoned discussions on the big issues facing the country. The Select Committee hearings on the News International scandal, particularly the contributions of Tom Watson, Paul Farrelly and Louise Mensch, show that parliament can do cross-party scrutiny when it so chooses.

Arguing for a new style of political discourse can lead to discussion on how we make our parliament more pluralist in nature, hence opening the door to consideration of the need to replace the winner-takes-all nature of FPTP with something better. There is therefore an opportunity to develop Miliband's language of a new politics into a debate that includes the need for a new voting system. In the aftermath of the referendum, simply asking people to support electoral reform is unlikely to take us far, but discussions on the nature of politics can lead Labour into a constructive, critical engagement with the means by which representatives are elected.

More directly, we can build the argument that support for electoral reform is good for Labour electorally. Just as it was polls showing that people were more likely to vote Labour if it supported change to AV that persuaded Gordon Brown to commit Labour to a referendum, so too we need to convince Ed Miliband and those around him that what they said about FPTP during the referendum campaign was not just right but also attractive to electors. Words, however, will not be enough – it will need reform-supporting organisations to commission the hard polling evidence.

A short word of warning: voters are quick to spot inauthentic behaviour in politicians. None of this will work if it is seen to be a tactical or opportunist stand, or if Labour were to talk electoral reform with the main motivation being to hoodwink liberal-left voters and Lib Dems. Offering nothing is a huge gamble on a quick victory under the winner-takes-all electoral system and, as we have seen, the odds of that gamble paying off are adverse. It would be much better for Labour to embrace and shape the change sincerely and willingly at an early stage. As a Labour supporter, I would rather the party did so than be bludgeoned into reform by four successive defeats or forced into something in hasty coalition talks.

Making Labour a national party

In several regions FPTP hugely disadvantages Labour. In Eastern England, the South East and the South West there is a substantial Labour vote but few Labour seats. The number of Labour voters in the East of England in 2010 was greater than the number in Wales or the North East – but their votes were rewarded with a measly two seats in parliament rather than twenty-six (Wales) or twenty-five (North East). In eastern England, having a Labour MEP elected by PR (Richard Howitt) has been a lifeline to the embattled party within the region.[70] The situation is not much better in the two southern regions (four MPs in each,

---

70 See Lewis Baston and Bob Blizzard, *How the East Was Lost* (2011) for more about Labour in the East, and John Denham et al., *Reversing Labour's Retreat* (LCER, 2007).

confined to urban exceptions, and not even an MEP in the South West).

This situation is not just bad for the Labour voters in the South of England. It is bad for the Labour Party as a whole. Labour's rules give a lot of power to the Parliamentary Labour Party (PLP), but this represents only the seats Labour won in 2010. Those seats are not the problem – under any mostly majoritarian electoral system (like AV or small-top-up MMP) Labour needs to have systematic input from the marginal seats it lost in 2010. Labour needs to understand the concerns of voters in the South, East and Midlands in order to make a meaningful electoral recovery, but the party's structures do not help this aim. Under Blair after 1994, the party got round this by centralisation and reliance on polling; but the party's appetite for centralisation and the leader's power to do it are both less in 2011. It is not a matter of neglecting Labour's heartlands; in order to do any good for the heartlands Labour needs to win the marginals. There has been an unhelpful dynamic in the past where parliamentary losses have caused the party to retreat into itself and ignore the voters. Giving a fairer voice for the South and East within Labour, and a fairer voice for Labour in those regions, is not only right in itself but a way by which the party can bring itself more rapidly back into election-winning condition.

The trade unions

Most unions affiliated to the Labour Party are not in favour of electoral reform, with the GMB (whose political officer is now the party's General Secretary) being particularly opposed. Strong supporters of reform within the trade union movement are few in number, although Billy Hayes of the CWU, and the non-Labour-affiliated civil service union PCS, are in favour.

The argument should be winnable within the trade union movement. Arguments that non-FPTP electoral systems are somehow too complicated for people to understand should not be able to gain much ground given that AV and STV are so frequently used in union internal elections. More politically, unions might ask whether electoral reform might enable them to achieve more of their policy goals. They should at least ask whether they can do better than the current system, in which Labour taps them for cash to spend on targeting the swing voters in marginal seats, in exchange for a few crumbs from the table.

For electoral reformers, any serious attempt to make reform a Labour project will have to involve a deep, continuing engagement with the trade unions. This requires a cultural change from reformers, who often come across as the sort of middle-class left-liberal who is uncomfortable with any form of collectivism and not very interested in economic justice.

Establishing links with progressive Liberal Democrats
In 1996 Labour, anxious to avoid yet another term of Conservative government, held talks with the Liberal Democrats (the 'Cook–MacLennan talks') which led to the manifesto commitments on the nature of the devolved assemblies and a referendum for Westminster. The co-operation was extended into government with a special Cabinet Committee during the first Blair term, which included Liberal Democrats.

With the Liberal Democrats in coalition with the

Conservatives, similar talks between the parties would not be possible at institutional level, but nevertheless there is a strong case for behind-the-scenes discussions, or even more open discussions between reform-minded backbenchers, over how the parties should conduct themselves if a hung parliament should arise. Such talks, which could include discussion of the preferred alternative to FPTP, could pave the way for the more formal coalition negotiations that would be necessary.

Ed Miliband's openness to some of these possibilities is welcoming and encouraging. The discussions with Richard Grayson (former Policy Director of the party) and other progressive Lib Dems should be continued, and be allowed to have a real effect on Labour's culture and policy. This is not only for Labour's sake in policy development, but also in order that the parties will enter any talks after the 2015 (or 2020) election with some bridges already built, and at least with some interlocutors who trust and like each other.

Something Labour can do immediately is reconsider its position on the government's House of Lords reform proposals. Satisfying though it may be to see Clegg fail, it is not mature politics on this question. No doubt the government plan is not perfect, but Labour should not oppose it. The government is intending to devote parliamentary time and political energy to finishing the Lords reform project that Labour started in 1997–99. It is the best chance we have of overcoming the Conservative Party's reluctance on reform and the inbuilt conservatism of the current Upper House, without spending any political capital on Labour's part.

Liberal Democrats

Electoral reform has always been a central plank of Liberal Democrat policy. The Liberal Democrats are major losers under FPTP and they know that they are unlikely to substantially increase their representation in the Commons without a change in system. There should not, therefore, be any great need for a major campaign to win Liberal Democrat support for electoral reform, although there will always be a need to reaffirm that support. It is a part of the core values of the party membership which, in the wake of the AV referendum and the leadership's absorption into a predominantly Conservative (and conservative) Whitehall, will need to be defended within the party. There is an important job for Liberal Democrat activists in making sure that electoral reform remains high on their party's agenda.

However, the Liberal Democrats must play their cards sensibly if reform is to be won, and do more thinking about the route to reform than was possible during the rapidly developing events in May 2010. Going straight for a referendum, and having a debate on reform that came from a cold start, did not work in 2011. Even in better circumstances than prevailed in 2010–11, it would probably still not work in the future.

Some of the more indirect and sophisticated options we consider in Chapter 7 may be of value, particularly a referendum on the principle that puts FPTP more on the defensive against the general argument for change. There is also the possibility of a citizen-led process (rather than a Westminster-led compromise) leading to a reform option, although this should be structured and involve different sections of society (as it was in British Columbia) rather than a voluntary effort bringing together the usual suspects. It also should not be perceived (by Lib Dems or by electoral reformers in general) as a betrayal of the historic aim of STV to settle for something like a simplified MMP (e.g. Total Representation), or even – if it really is all that can be accomplished for the time being – the Supplementary Vote.

A further possibility would be to have a citizen-led inquiry into the electoral system, or perhaps a more traditional commission of inquiry, plus a legislative guarantee that there would be a referendum within a specified timetable. After two very disappointing experiences (an open-ended commission of inquiry and a referendum that never happened from Labour, and a trap of a referendum from the Conservatives), the Liberal Democrats would be justified in insisting on a better deal in future.

As Mark Pack, not a habitual coalition critic within Lib Dem ranks, puts it:

> There should however be wide agreement on his [Grayson's] final point, which is that nobody in the Liberal Democrats should want working with the Conservatives to be the only conceivable option in the party's future. The question is more about what the best route is to avoid being trapped in a one-choice-only future.[71]

Many Conservatives would love to absorb the Liberal Democrats, as they did the Liberal Unionists and Liberal Nationals – and very nearly the authentic Liberal Party itself at its low ebb in the early 1950s. Not being beastly to Labour is not just the best prospect for electoral reform, but in the interests of the Liberal Democrat party itself.

71 http://www.libdemvoice.org/richard-grayson-ed-miliband-23033.html

Conservatives

While the electoral reform cause cannot expect support from the Conservative leadership, it would be a mistake to write off Conservative supporters for ever. Opinion polls conducted over the years have found many Conservatives – perhaps not a majority but a very significant minority – on the side of change. In the early months of the AV referendum campaign, up to 40 per cent of Conservative voters were considering a Yes vote. Their support may not be of much help in getting a referendum, but it could be important in winning it.

Very few Conservatives will not claim to stand for fairness: there is a job to be done in persuading more Conservatives that fairness can only be achieved by reforming the voting system. In 2005 when Labour won 55.1 per cent of seats with 35.3 per cent of the vote, and a comfortable majority in England despite being narrowly outpolled by the Tories, it was relatively easy. Unfortunately, instead of seeing the problem in the voting system, they chose – despite all the evidence – to regard the bias as a consequence of unequal constituency sizes, hence the legislation they have pushed through to narrow the range of constituency sizes. If, however, in the next general election Labour does better than them in converting votes into seats, they will need to face the fact that fairness needs electoral reform and there will be an opportunity for winning more Conservative converts. Perhaps if the coalition continues into the next parliament, Conservative culture will absorb more pluralist and democratic reforming values, just as it learned about capitalism in the 1880s and democracy in the 1920s from its ex-Liberal recruits.

Here we must pay tribute to the Conservatives'

electoral reformers. To support a position that conflicts
with that of one's party and to argue a case that most
colleagues bitterly oppose are not easy things to do.
The small group that has kept Conservative Action for
Electoral Reform going, think tankers such as Ryan
Shorthouse and Bright Blue, and MPs like Jonathan Evans
should be regarded as heroes of the reform movement
and must be encouraged and supported. Conservatives
such as Phillip Blond and others who are willing to enter
a thoughtful discussion of what electoral systems should
do, and what FPTP actually does, should also be valued
and appreciated.

Other parties

Like the Liberal Democrats, the SNP, Plaid Cymru, the
Greens and UKIP are strong supporters of electoral reform
of one sort or another. For UKIP, without a measure of
proportionality in the voting system, their chances of
winning the number of seats their support would appear
to merit are negligible (in 2010 UKIP, for example,
received 919,546 votes but did not win a single seat). They
are unlikely to have much of a role in any post-election
negotiations which could lead to a referendum, but come
the referendum their combined strength – 6.4 per cent of
the votes in 2010 – could make the difference between
winning and losing. As with the Liberal Democrats, it
will be important to keep reminding them just how much
they need a different voting system. The SNP, Plaid and
the Greens have a pluralist ethos at their heart. One of
many hugely disappointing results for Yes on AV was that
they lost the SNP vote. How this happened needs to be
examined. Far more than Ed Miliband, Alex Salmond

could have 'delivered' a block vote for Yes, but it clearly did not happen.

The 'democracy sector'

The 'democracy sector' (please, let us always keep those distancing inverted commas as without them the term evokes the smugness and exclusivity that reformers should abandon) badly needs to put its own house in order. There were bad relationships throughout the sector during the Yes campaign – between ERS and Unlock Democracy, between different bits of the ERS, between activists and central office ... the dysfunctionality of the Yes campaign brutally exposed the existing weaknesses of the sector.

Andy May, in his rapidly produced but thoughtful essay on what went wrong with Yes, has some thoughts about the future of the sector which should be considered and acted upon. A key paragraph reads:

> Some of the problems stemmed from the fact that the Yes campaign suffered from the inherent lack of transparency and the nepotism that afflicts the way long-standing funders and pressure groups in this area do things – the Rowntree Reform Trust, the Electoral Reform Society in particular. What I hope will come out of this account is a genuine conversation from the Electoral Reform Society and Unlock Democracy, the Rowntree funding body and activists from Take Back Parliament as how to become more professional, open, honest and accountable.[72]

Changing this established pattern requires more judgement

---

72 http://www.scribd.com/doc/55322336/Yes-to-Fairer-Votes-An-Insiders-View-published-on-Liberal-Conspiracy-http-bit-ly-lgw3Bk

and co-operation than we have been used to, and less insularity. But change is necessary. A healthy pro-reform sector is required to help create the next opportunity for reform, and to have the arguments and people in place to win next time. The state of affairs in 2010–11 let down a good cause.

Just as much as the political parties, the sector is dependent on a dangerously small number of sources of funding. The ERS depends on the profits spun off from its successful balloting subsidiary. Much of the rest of the sector competes for support from the Joseph Rowntree Reform Trust or, for things like research and education covered by charities law, the Charitable Trust. The concentration of financial resources gives a very few individuals enormous power within the sector as a whole, and even with the best will in the world this is an unhealthy situation. Pluralism is not just for the wider political world, nor are transparency or accountability.

Of the ERS, probably the less said here the better. It is a story for others with a neutral position and investigative skills to put together, not former members of staff whose perspective is inevitably partial. However, one may note in passing that for an organisation that is supposed to support clean, transparent politics its own governance falls far short of the ideal. Its internal politics were aptly described by James Graham as a 'nightmare'. Its governmental arrangements will be very difficult to reform, but reformed they must be. Its constitution is probably now more outdated than the United Kingdom's.

There are some strategic issues on which there may be genuine differences of approach. Different things can be accomplished by 'activism' and by insider lobbying and research, although the combination is more powerful than either alone. There is a risk in getting carried away with the positive experiences of activism and neglecting the need to build an intellectually compelling, tactically flexible case for change, and building alliances. The argument for change will not be won by waving pieces of cloth in Trafalgar Square, or another well-meaning initiative by centre-left celebrities.

There is also a question of what are valid issues on which to campaign. The ERS, by reason of its founding mission and its internal oddities, has always regarded the promotion of STV as being the overriding priority. The ERS, more than any other organisation in the sector, needs to be more relaxed about systems, particularly in a climate where there is not currently a House of Commons reform process. It is reasonable to examine priorities in the light of referendum defeat – and it was one of the frustrating aspects of working there that research not directly related to STV encountered difficulties and a lack of enthusiasm.

But the ERS needs to handle any broadening of mission carefully. Changing the electoral system is a focused objective, and the risk of broadening it is that it fractures a coalition. One may – as I do – support electoral reform but strongly oppose recall, for instance. Being pragmatic about electoral systems does not automatically mean signing up for a list of other constitutional reforms, or – as the ERS did during the AV referendum campaign – dropping any hint of criticism of whatever appears on the table. Rather than a search for trendy constitutional gimmicks like recall, the sector in general would be better off taking a step back.

The sector should also give up its distaste for party politics. Party politics is necessary for several reasons

– synthesising policy, structuring choice at elections, bringing forward leaders and organising Parliament, but reformers often talk as if it is abhorrent, or at best a necessary evil. If the sector is ever to accomplish change it needs to work with sympathisers (not necessarily yet supporters) in the political parties to give reform a distinctly Labour – and, who knows, eventually a distinctly Conservative – identity. Calling people hacks or dinosaurs because they are committed to a party's values is not helpful. Although the Liberal Democrats and smaller parties are staunch supporters, they are not enough to win.

There are conversations to be had with business, trade unions, advocates for women, ethnic minorities and the poor, and any number of other groups in society, but as long as the sector stays within its comfort zone these conversations will never happen. Unless another opportunity to change the political system is to be squandered, and the ideals and energy of so many good people are to be wasted, Andy May's conclusion cannot be bettered as a recommendation for the 'democracy sector':

Reform yourselves first – then reform the voting system.

Conclusions

In this book we have offered our explanation of why the
Yes campaign went so disastrously wrong. In places we
have been quite damning of the mistakes that were made
and of the failures of leadership that contributed to such
humiliating defeat. We take no pleasure in pointing out
these shortcomings – all who were involved in the campaign
were people who were committed to reforming our electoral
system. They had a difficult job to do and while we can
analyse their actions with the benefit of hindsight, they had
to react to the situations that confronted them and we do
not claim that if we had been in their positions we would
have got things right. We cannot, however, escape from
the fact that the Yes campaign failed miserably and that to
quite a large extent it had only itself to blame.

Of course we recognise that the campaign faced
experienced and ruthless opponents. The No campaign's
claim that introducing AV would cost millions, their
portrayal of AV as a system that was not just complicated
but grossly unfair, their distortions of facts and their
use of Nick Clegg's deep unpopularity among Labour
supporters all contributed to the campaign's downfall.
While recognising the effectiveness of the No campaign, we
cannot condone its tactics. Nevertheless, we must accept
that the Yes campaign brought about the scale of its defeat
upon itself.

› The assumption that a 'ground war' waged by groups of activists across the country could be a decisive factor in delivering victory was perhaps the most calamitous mistake, and if substantial resources were to be committed to local campaigning then much more needed to be done to ensure they were used effectively.

› The failure to reach out to voters using the freepost facility is difficult to excuse. While costs had to be considered, successful campaigning requires making choices between competing priorities and we question whether the right decisions were made.

› The attempt to run a political campaign without politicians playing a prominent part was misguided, and as a consequence the big-hitters, particularly on the Labour side, were not used as effectively as they might have been.

› The campaign was run with messages that did not resonate with voters, that in some cases were not credible, and that were not even convincing among campaign activists.

› The campaign appeared to lack people with sufficient political and campaigning experience, and there are questions over whether it had the management structure to make full use of the staff at its disposal.

However, even if fought and run differently, the campaign would have faced an uphill struggle in promoting AV in the political circumstances that prevailed in 2011. Firstly there was the problem of AV, an unhappy compromise that reformers had felt necessary to accept when negotiating with the dying Labour government. It offered a chance of movement on electoral reform, but was a system that could neither deliver the new politics people wanted to see nor fulfil some of the claims made for it during the campaign. Labour's defeat and a hung parliament should have been an opportunity for going for more, but the coalition deal sold reformers short. They were left trying to market an unexciting product.

That it had been negotiated by the Liberal Democrats who had done a deal with the Conservatives, however, perhaps sealed AV's fate. While Labour had pledged a referendum, AV was now a Liberal Democrat project. Liberal Democrat support for Conservative cuts and increases in university tuition fees made winning Labour support hugely difficult. Even if Labour had split down the middle, half of Labour plus the Liberal Democrats was never going to be as big as the other half of Labour plus the Conservatives – the sums simply didn't add up. The dangers of fighting a referendum under these conditions were then accentuated by holding the referendum on local election day when voters were more inclined to vote by party loyalty.

These problems might have been foreseen in the immediate aftermath of the 2010 election, but they were not. The pre-election Vote for a Change campaign and Take Back Parliament had created a clamour for reform and the movement's leaders were only too happy to seize what they could get. In the circumstances that, perhaps, was understandable, but the question whether a different approach might have persuaded the Liberal Democrats to hold out for more, or even for a different referendum date, will remain.

We now must look to the future. We have argued that with FPTP we can expect future hung parliaments and future coalition negotiations in which electoral reform will be a bargaining chip. We may not need to wait, as some fear, for a generation for it to happen again. But we see little point in running a repeat of the 2011 referendum unless we can change the arithmetic of support. To win, a proposal for reform must have much more substantial Labour support, and it must be a Labour project and not just a Liberal Democrat initiative.

To make that possible will require a lot of work. Labour must be helped to recognise that the chances of outright election victories are diminishing and that the future implementation of its policies is likely to require the support of others. Labour must be encouraged to discard its old tribalism and recognise that there are others with which it shares common ground on a whole range of issues. That will not be easy but, as we have noted, the effects and distortions of FPTP give plenty of scope for taking the argument to Labour members.

We have noted too that although changing how we elect our MPs might be off the agenda for a while, there are other ways in which the ground can be prepared. Campaigning for an elected upper house and for a proportional system for local government in England and Wales could do much to keep discussion of voting systems and how they affect the nature of representation alive.

Then there is the question of what should be offered as an alternative in a future referendum. The defeat of AV leaves open the possibility of a referendum on a proportional system, but full-blown proportionality, or even anything approaching it, is unlikely to be on the cards. We have avoided being prescriptive, but we recommend consideration of STV in small multi-member constituencies and of the newly proposed Total Representation system with a modest number of regional seats. Electoral reform purists might find these recommendations hard to accept, but if we are to make progress we need to find a proposal on which we can win.

Much of what we have written is an indictment of a poorly run campaign, fought at the wrong time and on the wrong issues. The message we want to leave, however, is one of hope. The campaign for AV was defeated, but not the arguments for electoral reform. The 2011 referendum was far from the first setback the campaign has suffered in its 150 year history. However, democracy, equality and the political empowerment of the ordinary citizen are, we devoutly hope and believe, an advancing tide. The intellectual case for reform which has been built by academic political science, and the campaigning work of organisations like the ERS, has created a position where FPTP is not used in newly democratising countries, nor even in newly created institutions in the UK. Another opportunity to rid ourselves of FPTP will surely come, and if this book has helped to increase the chances of success in the next referendum then we will be more than satisfied.

Appendix

Alternative Electoral Systems

Small STV (based on 2–3 member seats)

	Con	Lab	LD	Nat	Other
EE	33	6	19	-	0
EM	24	14	8	-	0
LN	27	31	15	-	0
NE	6	15	8	-	0
NW	25	35	15	-	0
SE	48	7	27	-	2
SW	27	6	22	-	0
WM	27	20	12	-	0
YH	20	22	12	-	0
England	237	156	138	-	2
Wales	9	19	9	3	0
Scotland	4	28	13	14	0
N Ireland	-	-	-	-	18
UK	250	203	160	17	20
Change	-56	-55	+103	+8	0
UK votes %	36.0	29.0	23.0		
UK model seats %	38.5	31.2	24.6		

Great Britain was divided for the purposes of the model into six single-member seats, 140 two-member seats, 106 three-member seats and seven four-member seats.

Using small STV seats gives surprisingly exact major-party proportionality on the basis of the 2010 vote distribution and assumptions about preference transfers. However, further research into the properties of the system is required before coming to any definite conclusion about its effect in other elections. In elections such as 2010, 1983 and 1987 where there is a large and evenly distributed Lib Dem/ Alliance vote it may end up favouring the party. Twenty-five per cent is enough to guarantee a seat in three-member STV and for a centre party that picks up transfers, in a multi-party system, it would often be good enough to win one seat in a two-member constituency. The Lib Dems would lose many of these seats with a moderate fall in their percentage vote. It is conceivable that Labour would have won an overall majority under small-seat STV in 1997 and possibly 2001.

The case for small-seat STV might look stronger after a 2015 election with a smaller Lib Dem share of the vote. The model result shows that in some circumstances it produces very close proportionality, which, while to committed reformers it is an attractive feature, may make it a step too far to qualify as a 'modest proposal'.

Total Representation

I have given a short description of the principles of TR in the main text. Here I will summarise the original version of the system proposed by its authors,[73] and some adaptations that in my view (not necessarily the view of its authors) would assist it in being implemented in the UK. The details are less important than the basic principle, which is that TR is a simplified version of a Mixed Member Proportional (MMP) system. The basic principles are very simple:

73 Aharon Nathan and Ivo Skrabalo, *Total Representation* (ERSP, 2009)

› Election for the majority of parliamentary seats in single-member constituencies using X-voting, as with current MPs in the House of Commons.

› Between 15 and 30 per cent of seats in parliament filled by 'Party MPs' in proportion to the total number of votes cast for unsuccessful candidates.

Votes	Seat 1	Seat 2	Seat 3	Seat 4	Seat 5	Seat 6	Seat 7	Seat 8	Seats	Vote
Party A	45	50	50	45	30	30	20	20	4	290
Party B	30	30	30	35	50	50	60	60	4	345
Party C	25	20	20	20	20	20	20	20	0	165

In this example, party A wins four constituencies and so does party B. How does one calculate who wins the two compensatory seats?

In the four seats (5–8) which A does not win, there are 100 votes for party A. In the four seats (1–4) in which B does not win there are 125 votes for party B. Party C has won no constituency seats and all its 165 votes are therefore in the 'pool' of votes for unsuccessful candidates.

The answer is therefore that party C wins the first compensatory seat and party B the next compensatory seat. Party C's candidate in Seat 1 fills the place, as she has the largest number of votes contributing to the pool of votes, and by the same logic party B's candidate in Seat 4 is also elected. The outcome is that party A has four seats, party B five seats and party C one seat. This is not proportionality, but does mean both that a smaller party with a lot of evenly spread support gets represented, and that the larger of the two main parties gets a bonus. The mechanism is simple – it means that instead of being thrown away, votes are 'recycled' – or, to use another metaphor, it is an each-way bet with a full pay-out for a win and then the hope of getting something back if your candidate 'places'.

Unlike STV, it does not completely eliminate the tactical vote, but it does widen the effective choices available to voters. It does have a slight tendency to over-represent marginal seats, because the candidates elected by the compensatory route will be those who also stood in marginal seats. Introducing it would be fairly incumbent-friendly.

The original model involves a system of designating constituencies which is based on more radical 'equalisation' than the government's policy and entirely mechanical criteria to eliminate gerrymandering. This may be suitable for Israel, but the use of local government boundaries, and an attempt to fit it to the map of communities, is firmly part of Britain's expectation of what constituencies should be.

The original version of TR involves allocating compensation seats at a national level; in a small parliament such as the Knesset, representing a small country, this seems logical. In the case of the UK and the idea of a strong local link in representation, it is probably appropriate to allocate compensation seats at a more local level. National-level compensation would involve a pretty low threshold for representation, giving MPs to more parties, while using the regions or countries involves more seats for the larger parties, including the overall election winner.

For the model, 111 extra seats (14.6 per cent) are awarded on the basis of the votes cast and seats won in the actual election, and the overall result then scaled back down to a parliament of 650 MPs. The D'Hondt averaging method is used, rather than the largest-remainder system as in the original version.

Model TR election result, 2010, using counties as the basis of the extra seats

	Con Actual	Con Add	Lab Actual	Lab Add	LD Actual	LD Add	Nat Actual	Nat Add	Other Actual	Other Add
EE	52	0	2	3	4	6	-	-	0	0
EM	31	1	15	3	0	4	-	-	0	0
LN	28	4	38	3	7	7	-	-	0	0
NE	2	2	25	0	2	3	-	-	0	0
NW	22	6	47	3	6	5	-	-	0	0
SE	74	1	4	4	4	9	-	-	2	0
SW	36	2	4	2	15	5	-	-	0	0
WM	33	3	24	3	2	5	-	-	0	0
YH	18	3	32	2	3	4	-	-	0	0
England	297	22	191	23	43	48	-	-	2	0
Wales	8	2	26	1	3	2	3	0	0	0
Scotland	1	4	41	1	11	1	6	2	0	0
N Ireland	0	0	0	0	0	0	0	0	18	3
UK	306	30	258	25	57	51	9	2	20	3
UK	336		283		108		11		23	
UK (scale)	287		241		92		10		20	
Change	-19		-17		+35		+1		0	

TR using counties or city sub-regions (compensation units of between seven and twenty-eight current Westminster constituencies) gives a result fairly similar to AV+ but via a much less complicated route. The voters' end of the process is the same as in FPTP rather than a complicated double-ballot of preferential AV and open-list PR as in the Jenkins system. It is majoritarian enough to give a party an overall majority in parliament when it is doing sufficiently well, and it does not do very much to make it easier for a smaller party to gain parliamentary representation of itself. However, the compensation seats do remove some of the disincentive for supporters of parties such as the Greens and UKIP to vote for their real first preference, and given that there seems to be a long-run trend towards smaller parties, this barrier may lower over time.

On the positive side for supporters of electoral reform, small-region TR has the systematic effect of making elections a bit more proportional (unlike AV, where this is contingent on other circumstances). It also has the benefit of doing something about 'electoral deserts' – areas of the country where a party has a significant vote but no parliamentary seats. Under this variant, there would be a Labour MP from Essex to represent the 157,134 Labour voters of the county, and a Conservative MP for the 121,131 Tories of South Yorkshire. Government and opposition would both be more representative of the spread of people who voted for them. The number of votes 'wasted' by the electoral system would fall sharply.

Using TR at regional level would mean UKIP gaining five MPs, so that its nearly one million voters would have something to show for their votes cast. The BNP would fall short of winning compensation seats on this model–although

Model TR election result, 2010, using the twelve regions as the basis of the extra seats

	Con		Lab		LD		Nat		Other	
	Actual	Add	Actual	Add	Actual	Add	Actual	Add	Actual	Add
EE	52	0	2	4	4	4	-	-	0	1
EM	31	1	15	3	0	4	-	-	0	0
LN	28	5	38	4	7	5	-	-	0	0
NE	2	2	25	0	2	3	-	-	0	0
NW	22	5	47	3	6	5	-	-	0	1
SE	74	1	4	5	4	9	-	-	2	1
SW	36	2	4	2	15	4	-	-	0	1
WM	33	2	24	4	2	4	-	-	0	1
YH	18	3	32	2	3	4	-	-	0	0
England	297	21	191	27	43	42	-	-	2	5
Wales	8	2	26	1	3	2	3	1	0	0
Scotland	1	2	41	1	11	2	6	3	0	0
N Ireland	0	0	0	0	0	0	0	0	18	3
UK	306	25	258	29	57	46	9	4	20	8
UK	331		287		113		13		28	
UK (scale)	279		242		95		11		23	
Change	-27		-16		+38		+2		+3	

they would probably have qualified if the proportional component were 20 per cent or over rather than the 14.6 per cent in the model.

Using national compensation would involve some fairly significant small-party delegations – eight UKIP MPs, four BNP and a total of three Greens.

Figures

The following pages feature the figures referred to in Chapters 2, 3 and 6.

Figure 2.1 shows public opinion during the AV referendum campaign November 2010 to May 2011. The data is compiled from various polling companies, who used the actual referendum question, via Anthony Wells's *UK Polling Report* (http://ukpollingreport.co.uk/av-referendum). Don't Know or Won't Vote figures fluctuate depending on polling methodology. Yes and No shares are expressed as shares of those decided and intending to vote. Last data point is the actual result.

Figure 2.1

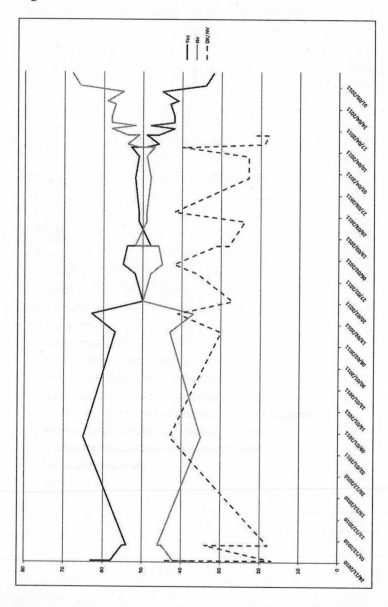

Figure 2.2

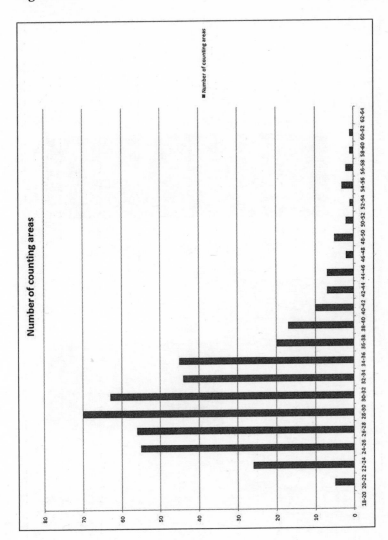

Figure 3.1

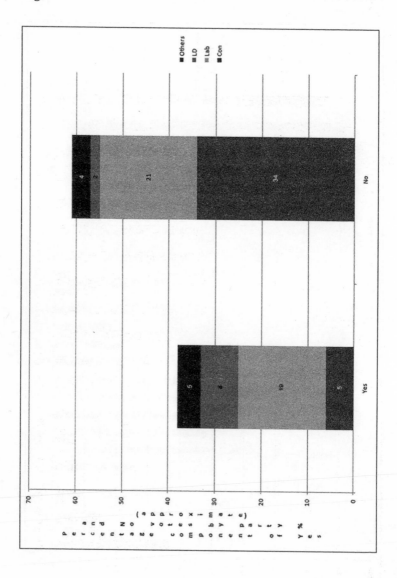

Figure 6.1

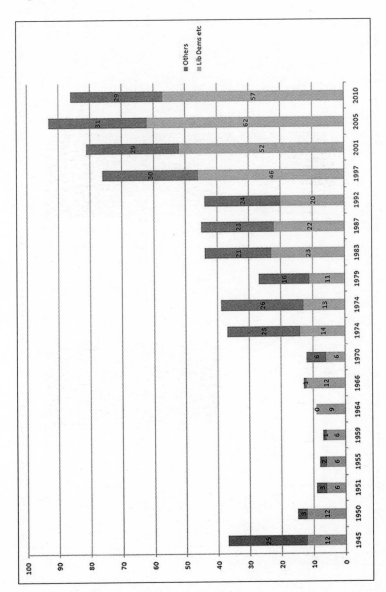

Figure 6.2

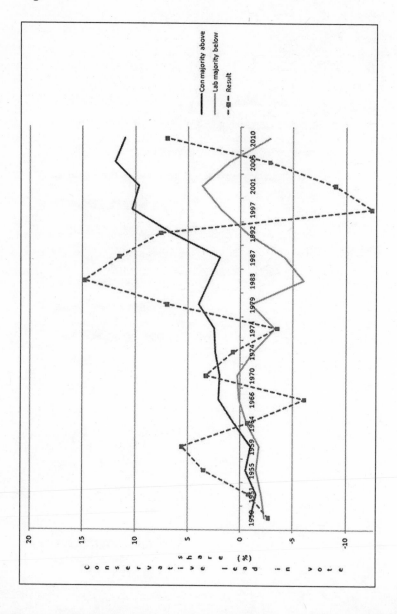